SURVIVAL ISN'T MANDATORY

OTHER BOOKS BY JANET PFEIFER

Our Silent Voice: Break the Silence

JANET PFEIFER

A MEMOIR

SURVIVAL

ISN'T

MANDATORY

Published in the United States by
Ignite Press
5070 N. Sixth St. #189
Fresno, CA 93710
www.IgnitePress.us

ISBN: 979-8-9850513-0-8
ISBN: 979-8-9850513-1-5 (hardcover)
ISBN: 979-8-9850513-2-2 (ebook)

For bulk purchase and for booking, contact:
Janet Pfeifer
jancpfeifer@gmail.com

Because of the dynamic nature of the Internet, web addresses or links contained in this book may have been changed since publication and may no longer be valid. The content of this book and all expressed opinions are those of the author and do not reflect the publisher or the publishing team. The author is solely responsible for all content included herein.

Trigger warning: this book contains sensitive topics such as sexual assault. If you or someone you know is in crisis, call 9-1-1 or the National Sexual Assault Lifeline at: 1-800-656-4673

Library of Congress Control Number: 2021920755

Cover design by Lindsey Bailey
Edited by Reid Maruyama
Interior design by Michelle M White

FIRST EDITION

IGNITE
PRESS
Fresno, CA

*This book is dedicated to my daughters, Stephanie and Katie,
who have grown into extraordinary women and are
the kind of mothers I wish I had been.*

It is not necessary to change. Survival is not mandatory.
— W. Edwards Deming

At the still point of the turning world. Neither flesh nor fleshless;
Neither from nor towards; at the still point, there the dance is,
But neither arrest nor movement. And do not call it fixity,
Where past and future are gathered.
Neither movement from nor towards,
Neither ascent nor decline. Except for the point, the still point,
There would be no dance, and there is only the dance.
— T.S. Eliot

"If we only have the will to walk,
then God is pleased with our stumbles."
— C. S. Lewis

Table of Contents

ACT I
Ready, Set, Go

Act II
If I Should Die Before I Wake

Act III
Keep Young and Beautiful

ACT I

Ready, Set, Go

One

The End

The Riverside Freeway was a sea of red tail lights and I prayed hard for an off-ramp to simply relieve my bladder. But I had to wait like every other commuter in this deadlocked mess. As the sun slid behind the Chino Hills, poisonous smog splayed brilliant pink and hot orange streaks across the sky. I was done fighting for the day and driving two more hours to L.A. wasn't a battle I wanted to fight.

As a Senior Project Manager, I had the job of convincing divisions of large manufacturing companies to implement quality specifications through every function and process in their facility. My logistics partner was sick, so I had the whole show. I felt pummeled after a hard meeting with line supervisors in a latch and fastener manufacturer in Riverside. I'd lugged my handbag — a rolling briefcase holding a massive laptop, binders of plans and spreadsheets — through security, across a hot parking lot to my car. I was done.

After ninety minutes of stop and go, I found myself in the same county as my parents. I calculated it would be smart to take the next exit to their house. I exited the filling station and walked to my black Volvo. I wadded up the paper towel, it arced and hit center into the trash bin as I muttered, "Wish Dad could've seen that."

I started the car and called Mom on the massive phone installed in my Volvo.

"My darling girl, I'd be thrilled to have you for as many days as you can stay."

"On my way as fast as I can." I tried to sound chipper.

"I can't wait. I'll make some cocoa . . . with marshmallows." A micro-vacation of chatting with my mother felt luscious as I inched my way to their house.

I was greeted at the front door with as strong a hug as Mom could give. She was thin from her struggle to survive the results of the 1962 surgical error that nearly killed her. And at this point she was getting all her nutrition from a tube. I felt her thin shoulder blades through her dressing gown and asked, "Where's Dad?"

"Oh, he had a teacher's union meeting at the school."

I rolled my eyes, and she laughed. Passion was the word my mom used. I used the words obnoxious and contradictory. We giggled together as we made our way upstairs to her bedroom, lined with pictures of my daughters, her favorite people in the world. Boxes of fan mail and love notes from her followers were stacked under the window.

"Mom, how is it, really?"

"Oh, I don't know," she said with some resignation. "No one can do anything, and I get so tired of battling the pain."

Twenty three years prior in 1962, Dad was under pressure to handle both the ham-fisted legal issues around my car accident and my mom's diagnosis of bleeding ulcers. He decided to take her to a small regional hospital while he traveled up the state to my court hearing in Central California. The local doc in a small Southern California town cut out her ulcer and left a rotting surgical cloth inside her, condemning her to years of pain and the agony of multiple surgeries. Her barely functioning intestines twisted in a growing web of scar tissue. Dad knew he'd ushered her onto this path of death and felt guilty.

She'd been required to go through repeated rehab programs to manage her "addiction" to heavy-handed pain meds. It was a silly exercise that left her in agony.

"How bad would it be to continue being addicted?" I asked this as I helped set up her pillows. She patted my hand as if my offered advice was precious but meaningless.

"I'll win this one sweetheart, count on it."

We talked about my job, and I showed her the pager I wore on my belt. My mother saw this stagecraft as proof her daughter had made it. I'm glad she was proud. We giggled with stories and she fell asleep to tales of her grandchildren and stubborn plant supervisors, resistant to the Total Quality Management changes being communicated by me, a woman who must be gay for some weird reason. She thought it was funny and gently chuckled.

I took a quick shower, made up the bed in my old room, and set the alarm. The end was near for Mom, so just in case, I prayed to our close family friend Jesus and pleaded for an end to the painful hell she lived in on this smoggy earth.

Dad came in from the garage and called, "Hey, Jannie." I shook off my sadness, went downstairs, and got swept up in the huge arms of my father.

"Pop — what's new on the union front?"

I loved his twisted logic, dramatic wafer-thin conviction, dipping in and out of politics, guns, religion, and worry about Mom.

"I'm getting out of this rat race," he announced with finality as we sipped leftover coffee in their olive green kitchen wallpapered with yellow flowers. I coughed at the bitter aftertaste of the lukewarm sludge my father loved.

"We're selling the house and moving back up north."

I gasped, "My god, Dad, what about Mom? A move will be brutal for her."

He shrugged as he walked back into the garage to get his papers and called over his shoulder, "I'm taking her to the mountains she loves."

Oh boy, this is tough. There is no hope for thoughtful planning. I want them to be happy, but dramatic explosion and spontaneous action with whatever was at hand defined our history. My stomach cramped.

I climbed the stairs and opened their bedroom door.

Mom said in a small voice, "My darling, come in, please."

She reached for my hand, and as I gently sat on the bed, she said, "It's for the best."

She knew the plan, and she'd left it for Dad to share.

Home in LA, I called Dad the next day and told him that I'd arranged vacation days to help with the move up north. He was thankful and told me when to be there. But Dad changed the schedule at the last minute without calling or leaving me a message. He hired a moving company, and it was nearly done when I got to their house. Mom was gone, in an ambulance to make the 230.6 miles alone, delivered to intensive care in another small town hospital in Visalia.

I frantically drove as fast as LA freeways would allow. The long trip ravaged her strength, and I was sure the drugs they gave her to ease her pain were too much. I had to get there fast. I arrived at the Kaweah Regional Hospital and faced a military response to my presence.

"Miss, you are?"

"I'm Janet, her daughter!" I said, my tone shaped into a short-tempered weapon. *Why is it always only me?*

Dad had forgotten to add me to the list of family members, answering their question, "Who are the family members," with, "I am. Her husband."

I was furious. I had to wait for him before I could see my mother.

I stood tall, thinking of what I wanted to say. Fury boiled inside my body, and I shook a little in front of this heartless soul behind the desk. "I'm sorry, miss," she said. "Do you have proof of relationship?"

Who carries that? I didn't carry the right proof of relationship? For God's sake, at our worst, we looked like twins! Take a breath, stay quiet, be polite, and say thank you. I naturally remembered the rules in response to anger, fear, and confusion when my small girl self was dropped off with strangers or was forgotten and had to find my own way home.

Dad was on the road, away from a phone, so I had to wait. I drank hospital coffee and skimmed magazines until he finally blew in. Not holding back, I broke into furious tears.

"Mom is in intensive care, and I haven't seen her yet. I don't know how she is because they won't tell me. I don't exist on their list of family members. They will tell only you because you didn't tell them you had a daughter!" My tone rose as the accusations flew from my lips.

"I'm sorry, Jannie." He said this like he'd been caught stealing candy.

I raged on through gritted teeth as he just sadly shook his head from side to side.

I stayed the weekend, and Mom woke up. We said goodbye, I wished her luck, and she rolled her eyes. I drove home through the San Joaquin Valley to Los Angeles. On my way, I stopped at the Cowboy Café, made some phone calls, cried in the bathroom, and hit the road.

Mom and I talked on the phone throughout the week. We spoke like everything would be just fine, and it was up to me not to worry. In time, she improved just enough to go to her new home. Dad had purchased a cabin in the woods just past the entrance to Sequoia National Park. This romantic vision — this house on a hill with picture windows overlooking the tree-covered, mountainous land — could only be reached by a single treacherous lane partially paved, up, down, around, then up again from the main highway in an area where it snows. He had to sell this house after the first winter. It was impossible to get in or out if Mom needed help, and the ambulance refused to negotiate the road in any weather.

Dad lost just enough of their money and said to me when I asked what he was going to do, "Don't worry, sweetheart, I made a special deal." Those special deals had never worked out well.

With my financial help, he found a little house on a hill up a big driveway, with a view of the river, in Three Rivers, the small town on the Kaweah River, on the main road from the San Joaquin Valley. That spring, Mom was rushed to Kaweah Delta Regional Hospital with a 104-degree temperature, nearly dying, and then barely reviving. When I called, the hospital gave me the news that she was slipping, and I drove up the state once again, wildly praying to be by her bedside. I practiced what to say if she could hear me. The last time I visited, she'd grabbed onto my arm and told me to clean behind the toilet. I wanted to get there fast, so the last words whispered in her ear were love — pure daughter love.

Mom died when I was just twenty miles away. I arrived, and her body had already been removed. She was gone.

Dad was with her body at the Webb-Sanders Funeral Home. In what was designed to be a soothing place, I found my six-foot-four father shrunk into a wet ball on a small spindly gold chair. There sat her weeping prince, grieving for his queen. My heart broke for him.

That Friday, my oldest daughter was graduating from high school. I picked up Mom's favorite dress and jewelry so she could be buried in style. I called a hairdresser that had been coming to their house to wash, dye, and style her hair. The hairdresser promised to polish her nails and make sure my beautiful mom would be perfect. I drove Dad to Southern California for my girl.

Mom was buried that June 1986. She was tucked into the family plots in Lindsay Cemetery, in the middle of acres of orange groves and under Kings Canyon National Park's glorious peaks.

In 1989, just under three years after my mother's death, Dad rescued a drunk, crazy woman off the street. He said God told him to, and bonus — he found a lady who drooled over his gun collection. He gave her access to my mother's Danish Modern dining room set along with her beloved rose-painted dishes. The sloppy drunk trashed it all. She smoked nonstop, got drunk weekly to the power of ten, and got mad. One night she shot her gun, then Dad got mad and fired his gun into the ceiling. She called the police posing as a victim, and they were both hauled off to jail. Years before, I'd engaged a lawyer to clarify power of attorney for health and property. She also became the "just in case" lawyer in town to protect me from the inevitable chaos he could cause. When I called her, she suggested I come up from LA to oversee the situation.

"No way," said I. "He did this, he's a grownup, the police have evidence, and he needs to take care of it.'

She took a long pause — I could hear a smile. "I know you're right. I'll call if any more crazy happens."

Oh my god, why me? Where's my brother when I need him?

Two

A Prince and the Queen

The story of my parents begins . . .

"People fill the streets surrounding Lindsay City Hall in hopes of catching a glimpse of the 1946 Orange Blossom Queen Ina Mae Redmond. At the height of the Orange Blossom Festival's popularity, it drew crowds of over 40,000 attendees, including radio, film and television celebrities."

I found this story on page 54 of Sarah Troop's book *Images of America: Lindsay*. The text is accompanied by a black and white picture of a huge crowd of people waiting. There are men in white shirts with rolled-up sleeves, women in dresses, some wearing hats, some not, all of them waiting. A young Hispanic man in the crowd looks sideways into the camera. Small children hang around on both sides of a restraining band of material labeled with the word CLEARANCE. There are kids on dads' shoulders, people milling, patiently looking, and waiting. They're all looking in the same direction. This mass of people is facing the direction of the early century, pale-colored City Hall waiting for the Orange Blossom Queen, the Queen, who will be my mother.

Lindsay is a small town in the San Joaquin Valley, nestled in the Sierra Nevada's western foothills. It's a little speck in the middle of California's long map, center east as you look from the Pacific Ocean across the state toward the range of mountains that separate California from everything else.

Our family migrated west to California around 1900. These people came for different reasons — from "snow sickness" to the freedom of living it up in the sun; from a profit-motivated desire to acquire land of lush and abundant produce to the desire of getting off the farm once and for all; from being dazzled by the San Francisco World's Fair to establishing churches and spreading The Word of God. After this familial migration, both my parents, Loren Shryer and Ina Mae Redmond, were born and grew up in this town. They watched their fathers grapple with service or not in World War I, attended small schools together, survived the same Great Depression, watched people flee the Oklahoma Dust Bowl dragging their starving families through the streets of their town, and yet, they were worlds apart.

In high school, Loren Shryer was a 6 foot 4 basketball star. His teammate and best friend was my mother's brother, Everett Redmond. Ina Mae Redmond was talented, athletic, strong, tall, and slim with glamorous wavy red hair and a dazzling smile. She was two grades below the two of them.

She had the best friends, the best grades, and the best-designed clothes. She and her talented mother made dresses, jackets, and pants from patterns they drew themselves. They'd buy movie magazines, *Photoplay* and *Modern Screen* at Tinken Drugstore to pick out fashions for Mom. She had a naturally voluptuous shape, and her clothing was tailored to accentuate her shoulders and slim waist. They made patterns with the bold colored fabrics Mom loved. She preferred to wear blue and green, colors that accentuated her golden eyes and red hair. They made removable pieces that could be washed by hand after each wearing then pressed for wear. She could dress up the same dress for an evening with a new collar, fresh underarm pads, gloves, and pearls. She worked on her make-up, so she looked dramatic. She posed in pictures, looking modern and sophisticated — on the leading edge, just like a movie star, confident and amazing.

I spoke with her two best friends soon after she passed in 1986.

These lovely elegant ladies, Janet and Cathryn, whose names I carry, loved to talk about their friend. "Your mother was such a star and the sweetest friend in the world," Cathryn said but lost her point once in a while. Her friend Janet filled in the spaces with ease: "Ina Mae and her mother were geniuses. They could make a dress just like it came from Los Angeles." I have pictures of these three in college. It seemed that looking like a film star was essential to the girls in this small rural town, just a few hundred miles north of Hollywood.

Mom was proud of herself. She said, "I was the Central Valley Singles and Doubles Champion. Not one player could return my serve." Posturing with the dust rag and broom, she was ready to be challenged by anyone on a Saturday afternoon of housework. I have pictures — triumphant poses with her partner and their trophies. An overachiever, the more she won and stood out, the happier she was. And, when she was happy, bluebirds chirped, the gloom blew away, the sun sparkled brightly, and the earth spun more smoothly.

As a child, I didn't realize the musical song I heard was from a narcissist. I was enthralled, tightly wrapped in her elegant, magical web. So was my father.

One night when I was in 8th grade, Dad tried to teach me math using poker. My mother played and sat on the other side of the kitchen table.

"She should have played poker in Vegas. She's the best cheater I've ever seen." He said this with glassy eyes and a look of total, mesmerized awe as she laughed and swooped up the winning chips.

While in nursing school, my dazzling poker-cheating mom sang for the wounded vets at the Oakland Naval Hospital while sitting on top of a wheeled upright piano. She performed the sad tunes and upbeat popular songs of the war-weary country as orderlies rolled her from room to room. The wounded veterans loved her. She dated a dashing paratrooper who became her fiancé.

An article from the Oakland newspaper's social page excitedly reports:

> *"Then there's Ina Mae Redman (sic) who decided a 'Guy*
> *Named Joe' was the man to pilot her future. She's flying high*
> *with a sparkler that resembles quite closely the Alameda*
> *Air Port (sic) giant landing spot. It happened Tuesday*
> *night and not before, even though I was informed she*
> *had been engaged over a year. They forgot people engaged*
> *a year generally walk with feet on the ground not just*
> *approximating it!"*

The fiancé was tragically shot out of the sky over the South Pacific in 1944, the same year of their engagement. Overcome with crippling grief, she dropped out of nursing school and went home. An article published in the hometown paper reads:

> *"Our sweetheart returns to the arms of her family to grieve*
> *for her hero, a brave paratrooper tragically shot out of the*
> *sky over the Pacific 1944."*

She spent 1945 suffering in public, and the whole town grieved with her. Keenly aware that a sad story had a short life span, she started to rebuild her stardom. She booked concerts around the valley while the town hoped and prayed for her. She sang and wept openly in concerts, at recitals, in church solos, and at gatherings thanking people for their loyalty and support. It was a brilliant PR campaign, and by 1946, she became the Orange Blossom Queen, her star rising out of the rubble of tragedy like a golden phoenix.

It was here, at this juncture, where her college roommate entered.

"My UOP (University of the Pacific) roommate had been scouted by a Hollywood actress and was going to be in a movie," Mom bragged.

"Meet me in Hollywood," her friend said, "it'll be so much fun!"

The audition was set with a big movie studio, and she knew this was her chance. Mom apparently took a deep breath, screwed up her courage, shook her hair, and made plans to move to LA and become a star.

At home in the Westwood Avenue house in town, Mom made lists, packed moving boxes, and shared verbal arrangements over Benny Goodman on the phonograph. Checking off her list, she moved with purpose. Her mother, Lalan Redmond, kept busy, fussing with Mom's wardrobe in the bedroom. "Hon, I think this little blue dress is just lovely."

Mom's father, Lester, gave advice from his brown leather chair, pipe held firmly in his teeth. He delivered a litany of warnings and "be carefuls" in his funny, over-exaggerated Maine accent.

In the middle part of this happy chaos came a knock on the door.

ᏓᏋᏋᏗ

On leave from his Army Air Corp Inflight Radar Repairman assignment in the Pacific Theater, my father, Loren, visited his parents Edna and Earl Shryer on the family's 26-acre orange ranch just outside of town. Over breakfast, in the spacious ranch house, Dad brought his father Earl Shryer up to speed on the war news, his dangerous job, the swift moves he made in deadly combat, the crashes, and the near misses in Borneo, New Guinea, and the China Offensive. His mother, Edna, interrupted to share some local news she'd collected. Who's who, the boys the town lost in the war, then she read the sad "our sweetheart returns" article aloud.

Dad put down his toast and coffee, got up from the table, dramatically grabbed his hat, and headed out the door. This extremely handsome boy, the football/basketball star of Lindsay High, had, at that moment, made the decision to rush to the Redmond's Westwood Avenue house to find out what was going on. He would change things, of course. He was impulsive, emotional, and usually made decisions that left heads shaking side to side.

Mom's father, Lester Redmond, and his brother Ray were the men behind Lindsay Iron Works, a thriving business. They made the tools needed to repair cars, tractors, and trucks in exchange for food during the depression. Man-hole covers on Lindsay's main drag, Honolulu Street, still bear the name of their company. These brothers were well-known in this small town. They were notorious. Lester drank, they were loud, and did things parents and grandparents were never specific about when I asked. I'm sure Lester fooled around. He had charm; he was well set in town, very good-looking, a champion motorbike racer, and the subject of widespread gossip.

Adding to the scandalous talk, Lester's wife, my grandmother Lalan, took a seemingly radical turn and converted to Catholicism. It was in response to the urging of her son Everett, my dad's best friend, my mother's brother. He was back from his WWII service on the deadly border between Burma and China, in the OAS (Secret Service), a shiny new passionate converted-in-a-foxhole Catholic.

It was too much for the Shryer's conservative, Protestant Brethren Mennonite family. For centuries the maternal side of my father's family protested against Catholic Papists, and this years-old protest fell on my mother's Redmond family in the succinct analysis of my powerful grandmother, Edna Pearl Mishler Shryer: "Those people are nothing but trouble."

That's Edna's short story about my mother's family. She usually added, "I told him to stay away from that girl. She will make his life miserable." When her strong Brethren sisters visited The Ranch, they agreed with her. They would nod solemnly and feel protective compassion for me, the surviving, wide-eyed child of this doomed couple.

It was a little true, but I didn't figure it out until I was almost nine.

After Dad flew out of the house, jumped into the car, sprayed gravel and dust in his wake as he drove away, my grandmother Edna, an amazing gossip, dashed to the phone and called a friend on the party line.

In those days, a call was made by picking up the handpiece. The operator would answer, and the caller told her who they wanted to talk to. She'd plug a wire into a switchboard and connect the call. This had a peculiar impact on gossip. If the operator was either friend or foe, she could stay on the call and say, "Oh my, this is good! I'll connect X so she can hear."

The operator helped that day by connecting other like-minded friends as they spread the story like flying monkeys. These friends complicated the juicy news with the involvement of the notorious

Redmond brothers. Word spread, and fantastically, curious people gathered in the streets to go to the Redmond house on Westwood.

ᴐℓᴐ

Just imagine a late afternoon sun streaming through a sliver of space between the top of a wooden window frame and a curtain rod in a simple little house on a tree-lined street. As the breeze ruffles the light homemade curtains behind the brown leather chair where Lester sits smoking his pipe, sunlight shimmers on the dust and smoke that floats in the house. The doorbell rings.

My mother, the soon-to-be movie actress, is annoyed. She swings her hair and announces, "I'll get the damn door." She runs from the bedroom to the front door. She opens to a man! Behind him, the sun shadows his face. He stands tall, breathless, hands at his side, handsome with intense smoldering dark eyes under unruly black hair. He's breathing deeply, his fit chest moving under his white shirt, tucked into khaki pants. His face has a glow of sweat and a look of abject adoration.

Behind him, a crowd of people stands murmuring, watching with the restless movement of a crowd's anticipation. Someone shouts, "Sweep her off her feet." Then a voice in the back calls out, "Marry her." The crowd gets a little restless, and he stands there, shoulders squared, feet apart, and mutely waits for the right moment. The afternoon sunlight bounces off his tall frame as his brow furrows over intense eyes. His breath is shallow, and the people behind him wait for the next part. They start a quiet chant. "Marry her. Marry her. Marry her."

Her life changes in a blink.

ᴐℓᴐ

I knew the end of this story, and each time she told it, she told it with flair, pictures, and treasures from her hope chest. As I got older, I couldn't quite figure out if she wanted me to feel sorry for her. A local crowd chanting "marry her" was undoubtedly intoxicating. In a magical visionary moment, maybe she saw herself as a glamorous wife with a handsome, tall adoring man and lots of little ones following her like ducklings. I also think being a big fish in a small pond was a more secure option than landing like a tiny anchovy in the Hollywood ocean.

Who knows, but from this set of dramatic and fateful choices, our life began.

Three

The Arrival

When my parents told the story of my arrival, they played it out like a motion picture.

The movie begins . . .

DISSOLVE TO:

EXT. LINDSAY MUNICIPAL HOSPITAL, CA — LATE AFTERNOON

It's August 18, 1947. It's hot and the San Joaquin Valley shimmers. Desert-like heat mirages rise from the streets below; beetles click, and locusts move their long legs in a rapid low tone. Birds sleep in the trees during the baking days and awaken at dusk. There's an irrigation haze hanging low over the valley.

FADE IN:

CAMERA STARTS WITH A LONG SHOT HIGH. SLOW SWEEP DOWN to a one-story hospital entrance. ZOOM to the entry over hazelnut and sycamore trees to the tall flag pole with a limp flag.

CAMERA SWEEPS RIGHT to the ER bay. Pick up the sound of the siren from the ambulance that has parked just past the doors of the ER. LAND THE SHOT DOWN even with the action.

The back doors of an ambulance open to attendants rushing to get a patient out while they shout to the doctor and nurses who are bursting through the doors of the ER.

A very pregnant woman is passed out on a stretcher with an IV connected to her arm, the fluid bag held high by a scrambling attendant. Several AMBULANCE ATTENDANTS race to get her carefully out of the ambulance, shouting to anybody in the vicinity.

AMBULANCE ATTENDANT #1. BP 135 over 90, pulse 92, seizure in transit, contractions 7 minutes apart.

DOC turns over his shoulder to his hospital staff as they run with the gurney to the back of the ambulance.

DOC. Call the OR. Prep for emergency C-section.

NURSE. Her BP is rising fast, probable toxemia.

One of the nurses turns and runs back through the doors. Running alongside the bed holding the IV fluid high over her head.

THE WOMAN on the gurney calls out in pain when another contraction hits, and her anguished voice is heard.

WOMAN. Call my husband!

DISSOLVE TO:

EXT. FIRE STATION, SEQUOIA NATIONAL PARK, CA -
LATE AFTERNOON (CONT.)

CAR CAM WINDS through Lindsay's back land; capture the
tan hills and green oaks of the low country roads through
Lemon Grove. Continue up the mountain road through
Three Rivers and through the gates of the park. WITH
A LONG HIGH SHOT, CAMERA PANS the terrain up the
mountain, focusing on the extreme switchback road.

CUT TO:

INT. FIRE STATION - (CONT.)

A phone rings. In the dining room of the fire station,
firefighters stop playing cards, making bad jokes, and
ribbing each other. They turn and look at the ringing phone
in anticipation. FIRE GUY #1 stands up, walks across the
room, and lifts the handpiece off the top of the black, wall-
mounted telephone:

He answers the call and listens:

FIRE GUY #1. Yeah, okay.

Holding the handpiece in the air, he yells:

Hey, Shryer, it's for you.

DAD looks up in surprise, jumps up from his chair, and runs
to the phone. He answers with a strong, definitive voice.

DAD. Shryer . . . What? (pause) . . . When? (pause) I'll be
    right there!

*He slams the phone down and turns, grabs the keys off the
wall hook, and starts to run.*

FIRE GUY #1. Hey Loren, what are you doing?

FIRE GUY #2. Are you crazy? Hey, what's going on? Is it
    your wife?

FIRE GUY #3. Loren, don't take the truck . . . you'll be in
    hot water.

*DAD rushes, grabbing his wallet, runs out through the open
fire station doors, jumps into the driver's seat of the red fire
truck, backs out, spraying dust, and turns on the siren.*

*The firemen run out of the station, falling over each other,
yelling for him to turn off the siren.*

*A CAR CAM follows DAD's wild ride down the mountain for
a mile or two. SWITCH TO HIGH CAM, with a soundtrack,
down the switchbacks, the fire truck horn blares when he
approaches then swerves around cars. The sirens fade as
he flies down the mountain and through the little town of
Three Rivers.*

FADE TO BLACK

FROM BLACK:

EXT. LINDSAY MUNICIPAL HOSPITAL CA - WANING
AFTERNOON SUN (CONT.)

HIGH CAMERA FOLLOWS the siren blaring fire truck as it arrives in the parking lot of the hospital ER doors. The sirens turn off.

The driver's door opens, and DAD exits with firefighter urgency, boots flapping, shirt leaving the confines of his pants. He sprints through the doors of the ER. CAMERA PANs OUT.

DISSOLVE TO BLACK

When I was born, Mom was clearly in trouble. She was ready to push, but her blood pressure was so high she was in danger of having a stroke. She'd had one seizure in the ambulance. When doctors got her into the ER, they had to relax her body, and she was given a shot that included curare. Used by South American Indians, curare is the poison placed on arrow tips to paralyze enemies who'd then be captured and eaten. That was not a specific drug-related side effect for Mom, but momentarily paralyzed, she stopped breathing and had to be resuscitated as she was rushed into surgery.

My entry was fast and dangerous. Not breathing, knocked out by Mom's anesthesia, I was rushed out of the operating room while she lay dying behind me. A doctor whisked me away from my mother, held me upside down, and smacked my feet. I frowned and stopped breathing. The doctor ran down the hall; loose wrapping blankets fluttered as he rushed by my father holding the baby and said, "needs to breathe . . . "

It was almost too much for my waiting dad, in a bare room lined with sharp armed chairs as the perfume of antiseptic slowly circulated around his sorrow. Submerged in fear, prayers were the only life jacket keeping him above hellish depths. Time slinked around the shock of losing both the woman he loved and his baby boy.

An exhausted surgeon pushed through the hallway doors, wiping his hands on a cloth. His scrubs were randomly spattered with blood.

He reported, with a chilling lack of detail, "There was too much blood." He stopped and looked right at my dad.

"There might have been a stroke. She stopped breathing. We have to wait and see."

The doctor turned back to surgery as Dad's face strained into a frown. I can imagine his dark brown eyes darting right then left and filling with tears as he stared into space. In the waiting hours, an imagined world of being a dad with a beautiful wife and noisy family slowly twisted, curling in and out of reality as those imagined voices slowly rolled into a silent scream.

Suddenly, a nurse came around the corner and smiled. She said in a sunny voice, "Eight pounds, four ounces. She's had a little trouble breathing but everything looks good for her now. Oh, and your wife is doing well, too!"

"She?"

One baby, a girl, snuggly wrapped in a pink blanket.

Four

The Still Point

When asked by damp-haired grandchildren to tell a bedtime story, I told the story that made them roll with laughter.

When I was very little, I stood at a locked screen door in the bright light of early morning. Sleep-messy blond hair topped the head on my small frame draped in a rumpled nightgown loosely hanging over sagging diapers. I fixated on a dog. His ginger-colored, furry head was up, ears pricked to attention, eyes down, one paw in the air as he lowered his nose to investigate a stink bug on the sidewalk. This spectacle played out behind the veil of rising mist from water shot by a lazy sprinkler. The bug raised the back of its carapace and released the stink it's named for. The dog yelped and frantically rubbed his nose on the grass, then jumped straight up and down, shaking his head. I was thrilled, lost in the comedy, when the sudden feeling of something warm and wet escaped my cloth diaper and puddled at my feet. I knew I was in trouble, and my grandchildren think a kid standing in a puddle of pee is hilarious.

I grew up with a clear understanding of right, wrong, good, and bad, but how did I know trouble when I was just a baby? I didn't even have the word at that age.

When I asked my mother how I could possibly feel I was in trouble, she said I was being dramatic. Avoiding the question by assigning unnatural behavior to a little kid in diapers looking at a dog and a stink bug, she said, "Don't be silly, my darling girl, you were almost trained, and I'm sure you weren't in a diaper."

My mother believed that her daughter, who walked at nine months, gave her bragging rights and used this improbable achievement as the *pride of ownership.*

"My child is remarkable. She walked very early, imagine this, at nine months, and was toilet trained before she was one." She added, "Not like most children." When my mother spoke of "her daughter," which she did until I was married, it never felt like the real me.

For the first four months of my life, both sets of grandparents shared the nurturing, feeding, and care of their first grandchild while Mom recovered from her surgery. My parents lived in a vacant lot across the street from La Verne College, a Brethren school founded by my great-grandfather Jacob Mishler, Edna Shryer's father. Their house was one in a string of Quonset huts, World War II temporary housing for returning vets. Dad was getting his degree in history and his teaching credential, while Mom planned her next rise to fame.

Part of her history included the complaint that she was set back by marriage to my father and had high expectations of her child. She knew how to gain fame, and nothing was going to stop her. She could use her near-death experience and the setback of marriage to fuel her journey to stardom. Later in life, she was called "brave" despite the so-called barriers to her trajectory. One of those barriers was getting stuck back in small-town life. She was convinced she deserved better if only . . .

Delivered into the arms of my parents, I was four months of chubby cute, and she had a plan for training this girl of hers to shine as the prime example of her brilliance . . . her very well dressed, well behaved, completely toilet-trained by year one, reading by three, singing on key, walking-early child. With more than a few puddle-making dirty escapades, I was molded into the reflection of her success as a mother. Pride drips out of my baby book. What else would you expect from the child of Ina Mae Redmond Shryer?

When she recovered, she started to sing. The newspaper articles crow about how her "personality filled every available space," and people in the small towns of eastern LA County fell in love with her. She became almost famous. It took diligence, discipline, organization, lists, and endless energy. She did her best to become the dazzling one, desired, her name growing bigger with each concert, wedding, funeral, and theatrical production. She did well in this new pond. "Celebrated" was the word she loved to hear.

My father, the after-school animal catcher, was an athletic La Verne College football-playing specimen. He was the picture of a 1948 returning soldier, thin from youth and the rigor of war and muscled from hard work. His short sleeves' cuffs rolled up over his muscles, and his dark hair looped over his deep-set eyes; he was the best looking guy on the crew. His job, however, was a problem for his shaky sympathy button. He brought his ragged catch — cats, dogs, possums, and birds — to the Quonset Hut row before they went to heaven through the efficient gassing process of the local pound. Both my parents treated the arrival of animals with excitement, and it worked. My mother's idea of good parenting was to give each animal a name before they went to the pound, so they became angels rather than unnamed, doomed meat. This twisted logic of naming animals stuck with me and soon I was naming everything that moved.

A very special rescue was a bird. Not only did this grey cutie fly down to dance with me to the music of my little record player, but the bird also manipulated all of us. It could talk and, when it crooned, "Hey, Ina Mae," my flattered mother declared it part of the family. I was eager to give it the best name to save its bird-soul. But, fascinated with the bird's elimination splats on the newspapers under its perch, my mother saved us from my idea of a name. "Potty-Poo" was abandoned, and she called him The Bird after Charlie Parker, a famous jazz musician whose LPs regularly played on our turntable.

One afternoon when Dad's truck stopped in front of our hut, he called to my mom, "Hey Ina Mae, come out here and bring Janet."

He opened the passenger door, and a ball of fluff jumped out. It was the cutest dog in the world — curly-haired, black and white. He trotted up to me, sniffed, sat, and just looked at me with huge brown eyes. Dad said, "I think this is a smart one."

My mom said, "We'll see about that — where did you find him?"

"On campus, over by the gymnasium," Dad said with a proud smile.

Mom stood over the dog and got his fluffy, big brown-eyed, happy tail attention and warned him with authority and strength, "I could give you away, mutt."

I named him after a fence. Picket, this perfectly named dog, was mine. Neighbors took pictures of our silly, wound-up team on leashes: Picket and me, the wild ones, wet and dry, sagging britches and muddy paws.

After Dad graduated, my great-grandfather Jacob Mishler gave us a car. Dad started teaching sixth grade at a local grammar school, and Mom got pregnant. It was time to move.

While buddies helped my parents pack and load, my mom thought it was funny to tease me as Picket barked and ran between the moving truck and me. She tried to give my dog away to the students, "Hey, you can have this . . . mutt!"

She drove me crazy. She'd secured my stealthy body to the front porch of the hut with a rope tied to my pants. I had access to a sandbox, where I worked out my I'm-tied-to-the-porch fury with revenge "No, No, No!" With all the necessary tools to build a kingdom and a water hose to bring an imaginary storm, I planned to take out the town. Fables and stories fed my imagination. They played on my tiny record player while Picket napped, and The Bird and I listened to the story of the Pied Piper of Hamelin, who led children away from their families into a cave, and girls with long blond hair were held hostage in a tower by an angry witch. I was the witch over the town in my sandbox. My mom heard me talking out the childish story of anger and doom as she carried boxes and lamps to the truck.

We moved into a tiny guest cottage on a grassy green hill in San Dimas on Van Dusen Drive behind Mrs. Hosford's Craftsman style two-story house. The Bird went to Mrs. Hosford, and they were made for each other. When I stayed with her, The Bird kept me within voice distance while I marched around her house, which was as big as a castle. This hill was beautiful, full of wonder, avocado trees, California pepper trees, sycamores, endless space. And a kingdom of gophers.

Mom was so happy to move into a real home, and she began to demand the family piano. Our family's upright grand is a Wing and

Sons mahogany instrument with ivory keys and five pedals. It arrived on a train from Maine and arrived in San Francisco before Mom's Redmond family landed on their westward migration to California. It was in the living room of the Redmond's Westwood house in Lindsay. My sweet grandmother Lalan won it in a contest between her and her sister-in-law. My great-grandfather Horace Redmond came up with the devilish competition, won by my grandmother, who played a scherzo. Lalan came from a family of fourteen in Tennessee. Her father was a teacher and school superintendent in the rugged reconstruction years following the Civil War. Nathan Scott and Nancy Caroline Anthony had twelve children who each had to master an instrument. I remember a long-lost picture of the family "Orchestra" in front of their barn in Franklin County. Years later, while Lalan, the ninth daughter of Nancy and Nathan, and I, a high schooler in the 1960s, washed dishes, I told my darling Lalan how proud I was of her for winning that contest. She laughed, sweetly taking no credit. She then lectured me on the danger of pride, one of many deadly sins. I immediately thought about her daughter, my mother, and wondered if there was a hidden message.

∽∾

In 1950, my uncle Everett and Dad rented a truck and drove 392 miles round trip to get the piano for my mom. When they arrived, I was safely tied to the water spigot. These two huge, strong, sweaty men moved the piano into the cottage through the narrow doorway. When the piano was finally leveled on the floor and sound checked, Uncle Everett untied my "safety" rope and picked me up. Dad popped some beer bottles, and Mom sat down, grinned with glee, and started to play ragtime with gusto, wincing with every out-of-tune key. Picket sat on the front step on the other side of the screen door, lifted his fluffy chin, and howled hard. It was the sound of my childhood: Mom on the piano, singing and playing to her heart's content, and Picket singing backup.

The operatic black and white dog found his destiny on this hill of endless gopher trails. His job, we all agreed, was to rid the hill of these little brown rodents, and his routine was fascinating to watch.

His head would tick just a bit, not a hair of movement for several long minutes, before his eyes focused on the ground until the gopher stuck its head out to check the scene. Silently he'd lift his body on two hind legs, pounce, and *wham*! Picket would snap and catch — a blur of dog and squishy gopher. I made loud pronouncements, marching, yelling, avoiding the carnage, and making messy mud piles beside my best friend, the prolific gopher killer. We must have looked like wild aliens as dirt hurled higher and higher. I snapped flower petals and stripped fern fronds from Mrs. Hosford's garden.

My mother caught us and sternly reprimanded us as Picket hung his head, and I cried. She picked up squishy bodies and made us clean up and apologize. Mom had a picture of us standing on the front porch of Mrs. Hosford's house with Picket by my side. We were covered in the evidence of our destruction, guilty and mad. I imagine both these adult women had their say about our behavior.

"You were so funny," Mom told me years later as we watched my little daughter in her backyard. Taking off her sunglasses, she mused, "While you were fixing what you and that mutt messed up, you'd copy my scolding — nearly word for word. You were such a smart little thing."

The early part of my life was filled with magic that happens at the still point of time, with no beginning and with no end. My mother loved musicals, and she acted as a stage manager in my life. With the talent and energy of a self-declared celebrity, she produced movie-worthy holidays. I loved and believed every one of the magical numbers where her child was the awe-struck believer. She told these stories to me, her friend's children, and my children. Almost always the emphasis was on the brilliant director.

∽ℰ∽

One Easter Sunday: On a sunny April day, our girl awoke . . .

. . . climbed out of her crib-bed and rushed, dragging her blanket, thumb in mouth, to the front door. She couldn't reach the handle but knew something magical was there, on the other side. She knocked on the door from the inside, and Picket, the black and white dog, barked outside. Jumping up and down in her bare feet and nightgown, a blanket sloppily wrapped around her warm little body, her blond hair sleep-tangled, she was breathless with excitement. The door opened slowly, and she gasped at the bow-topped basket filled with chocolate and colored eggs. Her gaze landed on the plate next to the basket. Two green-topped carrots had huge gnaw marks! She could not believe her eyes. On the path leading to and away from the front door were white bunny footprints, leading to and away from the carrots in the dish, the spot around the Easter basket, and off into the grass . . .

I have to say it was the Easter Bunny myth that I remember having a hard time giving up. The theatrical way my parents moved through life fell short in real life, where I had to survive. My assigned role was to deliver a set of predetermined, status-laden accomplishments.

෴

One sleepy afternoon, several months after we moved into the cottage on the hill, Mom took time for a nap and asked me to join her on the big bed. She made a noise and asked me to feel her tummy. The movements of my new brother or sister made me still and quiet as it did for my girl when I was pregnant with her sister. My mom made it exciting to talk and sing to our newest family member. We thought up names. If it was a boy, he would be named John Wesley, after my dad's grandfather. If it was a girl, she would be Abby after my mom's great-grandmother, Abby Fields Newcomb. Mom told me the new baby would sleep in the dresser's middle drawer until we moved into a bigger house. I can smell that warm afternoon in crisp sheets dried by the wind. I was happy, filled with glee, looking forward to our baby as we read magazines and napped in love, naming my brother or sister in the afternoon sun.

When Mom was rushed to the hospital with the first dying baby inside of her, all I remember is being taken to Mrs. Hosford's house in the middle of the night. I can still smell that cold night air. Damp grass, soft dirt, and pepper trees let off their sharp, sweet smell as Dad's running feet broke open the seeds. He carried me in his arms, Picket close by our side as we rushed down the hill. Holding tight to my blanket, being in Dad's arms, I felt the wonder of a dark, star-filled sky, having never been awake that early.

I was too little to know that life could stop and change forever.

Dad came back to Mrs. Hosford's house, picked me up, and took me to the hospital to get Mom. I was barely three years old. Waiting in the hallway, I'm sure I fidgeted endlessly. I was too young to be quiet. I knew my mother was behind the closed white door. My memory of that time is bits of vivid scenes, but my parents perpetuated the story that included my loud, nonstop desire to dance and sing, asking "why" over and over again. I was ordered to be quiet and still. This was serious. I had to wait. For a little girl, waiting and worrying are noisy.

$\sim\!e\!\sim$

I'd heard leather shoes, hard heels clicking on shiny polished linoleum, but then, when I was little, the footsteps belonged to the chilling sight of a white-coated man walking toward us. Dad said I "stopped cold."

The man and my father had a quiet conversation standing up. I looked up and saw moving lips and hands, nodding heads. Not a shock yet. Then the man turned his head and looked down at me. He started to kneel down. The crinkle of a starched white coat and the black holes where his eyes should have been triggered the thought of "monster." His huge hands cupped my small face. His nose was big, his breath smelled like old coffee and a pipe. He said in a strong whisper, "Your mommy is not going home. It's time for you to be a big girl *NOW*." As he said "now," his finger poked my chest. He must have seen tears because he added, "No tears. No crying."

My body was stiff and immobile. I don't think I was breathing.

Sounds changed, and my heartbeat got loud.

I had to be big. I had to stop crying. I had to be big.

I had to sit still in the car with my dad; there were no seat belts, and he couldn't hold me with his arm. He was crying. I knew something bad happened. We stopped at a house I'd never seen before. We walked up to the front door. Dad rang the doorbell and looked down at me. A pretty woman opened the door, and in whispers, they talked about my mother, and then I heard him say, "I can't take care of her."

Immediately, my world shrank into a small ball that might roll under a table, into a corner, in the shadows . . . to escape . . . to disappear . . . .to be safe.

The lady took my hand and led me into the house. I looked back at my father walking away . . . I'd been given away. I knew what that meant and thought about the pound. I didn't say a word, I didn't look up, I didn't speak, I was mute. The sound around me was a low wattage hum. My mother wasn't coming home, my father left, and I was with a woman I'd never seen before.

My dog was gone.

The Bird was gone.

My mom and dad were gone.

She led me into the kitchen and asked if I wanted something to eat. Quiet.

She showed me to a bedroom and helped me up on the bed. Quiet.

I cried myself to sleep. Quiet.

I held on to my resolve to be as big as big could be. Being big took my mind, robbed my voice, pained my heart, and made me tired.

My father returned that night with my things in a brown paper bag. I awoke, sat up, and listened to the hushed conversation. Quiet. I remember hearing the lady's irritation about me not eating. "What am I supposed to do?" . . . "What does she eat?" . . . "She just sits there or leaves and takes a nap."

At my dad's gentle laugh, far from the bedroom, I heard him say, "She'll eat when she gets hungry."

He left, and the car sounds got faint as he drove away. I was small and hurt. I slept to disappear — two or three times a day.

The lady polished my shoes. She reminded me that she'd shined them and that I should be happy. A child given away like a puppy was supposed to be happy? I had the wrong feelings?

My clothes were always clean and pressed. She talked nonstop, worrying I'd lose weight and my father would think she didn't feed me. I sat in her big flowered chair in the living room. The chair faced the window, crisscrossed with white ruffled curtains, to the front yard and the street where I got out of the car. I sucked on lemon drops from a pink dish on the side table. My neat, polished shoes and white socks just came to the edge of the pink-flowered seat.

The lady talked and talked as she dusted. She said things like, "He left you here longer than he promised," and "It was time he took care of his own daughter," and "He should have told me you'd be here for more than a couple of days."

She talked until I got tired. I slipped out of the chair, walked away, and took a nap. Empty.

One day, my father did come. He quickly shuffled me out of the house with apologies, clothes, and a toothbrush stuffed in the wrinkled brown paper bag. As we walked to the car, she called out to my father that I never spoke a word and that she tried to feed me.

He laughed and said — "She is *such* an actress." He was talking about someone else, not me. They didn't know how terrified I was thinking that he'd forgotten me. Given away . . . lost and left behind at a stranger's house? He didn't know I would never be the same? I broke.

∽ℓ∾

Several months after my mother died in 1986, my dad and I played a round of golf in Three Rivers. We were talking about Mom, and I asked him about that day. "Pop, remember when Mom lost the baby, and you picked me up and said . . . "

He didn't let me finish the sentence. He stopped in his tracks and turned to look down at me. As tears started to rise in his eyes, he said, with a straight face, looking at his professional, adult daughter, "I remember every last minute of that time. I lost my son!" He sounded like he was accusing me. He took a breath, "Your mother didn't want to live." The last words were spoken in a talk-yell. As I waited, calming my heart rate, he brushed his tear-filled eyes and took a breath. His voice rose to the last words of his sentence, he sputtered, "You were lucky to live. Do you remember how rude you were to that lovely lady who took care of you? How you scared her with your theatrics, your . . . your little play?"

I could barely breathe. Leaning on my club to keep from falling, I said quietly, "Dad, I was not even three, and it was shocking. I even remember the smell in her house."

Our golf game got very odd, the two of us squaring off in our interpretation of a day 35 years in the past. I stammered, and as I took off my sunglasses, I shakily said, "But I was little . . . "

He cut me off, "You were smart." He yelled at me, "You knew exactly what you were doing — not talking, scaring us all to death."

I could not believe what I was hearing. Dad talked about me as if I'd been an adult when I wasn't yet three years old. I could not come to grips with how bone-crushingly sad it was. At that moment, with the sun setting over the hills in the west and casting an amber glow over the 9th hole, I looked at my dad and knew I lost this parent when my brother died.

Throughout my young childhood and until I got into high school, I awoke from two nightmares in tears, covered in breathless sweat.

◡◡◡

I'm shown to a door by an adult with an understanding that there is a place to nap in the room on the other side. I'm so tired I could sleep anywhere. All I want is a bed. The door opens, and I see a white room lined on both sides with colorful fluffy beds with lots of soft pillows. When I go to the side of a yellow bed and look for a way in, I see that the bed is a sardine can, open with high, razor-sharp sides. I try to think of a way in — knowing I'll be sliced to pieces if I try. I look for help, and there is silence.

◡◡◡

In a very high hospital bed connected by needles in my arms to Kool-Aid colored liquid-filled tubes, I'm screaming. In my dream, I know my brother is somewhere, and he can help. I plead with faceless people who come into the room. They ignore me. I rip off the tubes and run as fast as I can, knowing he's there, down the long white hallway trying to open endless locked doors, then wake crying, wishing my brother could hear me.

ᔆ

I naturally asked my mother about that time as I grew into a world of social norms. Every kid I knew had brothers and sisters, and I was the only single kid in school. She'd weep and give in to the silence of grief, trying to control her tears, before she would talk about the details. She did chuckle about Picket going on overdrive to make her happy. When they got home from the hospital after losing the baby, the fluffy killer had decimated the rodent population on our hill and stacked piles of mangled, dead gophers on the front porch. Dad had to collect the chewed-up bodies and take them to the dump. He said Picket proudly sat solemnly by his side in the front seat, fluffy chin held high — a job that had to be done.

When I came home from the stranger's house, I sat with my blanket and a book on the couch. I have a picture of that day; it is bizarrely cute. I don't look damaged, but my face is serious. Picket sat on the front step outside the screen door, howling while my mother played the Moonlight Sonata and cried. The baby was my little brother. He took one breath and died. My mother told me that she didn't name the baby, and I didn't tell her that I took care of it in a prayer when I was little.

His name is John Wesley.

Five

Ice Cream, Cowboys, and the Circle of God

-1951-

Mom started to feel she might lose the second baby after she lost the feeling of fluttering life. Mom told Dad to take me to our family. She'd got a call from the lady Dad took me to when my brother died. Mom was not happy and wanted me to be with people who loved me. This trip's plan was for my great-aunt, my grandmother Edna Shryer's youngest sister Almo, to care for me for a couple of days in Los Angeles then drive me to the family ranch in Lindsay. I would stay with my grandparents at The Ranch until my parents were ready for me to come home.

Great-aunt Almo and Uncle Chuck had a brick house on a hilly, tree-lined street in Burbank, California, a suburb of Los Angeles. Chuck was a popular dentist with landholdings both in Los Angeles and the central San Joaquin Valley. The driveway was designed with bricks and squares of grass, perfect for an imaginative four-year-old. It angled up a small hill from the street and went all the way to the backyard. One day, something scared me.

-1993-

Marsha's voice on the sound system quieted the crowd. "Now, ladies and gentlemen," she began, "we've all grown up with the story. That special story of little Janet." Low loving chuckles came from the audience, from people who adored her and her mother.

Marsha was my cousin, tall, commanding, and admired in the Masons and Eastern Star organizations. She and her mother Almo were legends in the community, and I got a little star power when I stayed with them. Marsha was dedicated to putting on a big show, and on this August afternoon, in the VFW Hall in Lindsay, the show was about her mother's sister, my great-aunt Flossie. It was Flossie's 100th Birthday.

I didn't see Marsha turn and grin at me, but my father and daughter did. Katie leaned over the table and interrupted my conversation with Flossie's grandsons Craig and Doug, and said, "Psst. Mom, I think cousin Marsha is talking about you." I looked up. My dad was laughing, his hands covered his face, and his shoulders shook. Confused, I turned and looked at the stage, and Marsha announced, "And she's here! Janet, come up and tell us the story!!"

I don't know how long the seconds dragged before I registered that my oddball cousin was gesturing to me like a bus driver urging a late rider to hurry up. People were clapping and nodding in agreement, but at that moment, I had no idea what she was talking about. I mouthed to my dad, "What the hell?" and he just shrugged, wiping his eyes. My mind reached for the right thing to say. I looked at my daughter, who was doubled over in laughter with my raucous man cousins at the table. They were cheering rodeo style, watching the girl they used to torment, walk up the steps. They cupped their mouths so the sound would travel and yelled, "You've done it now, Janet, we will never let you live this one down! Ha ha ha, whoop, whoop!"

Marcia's face was radiant with high expectation as I took the mic. I reached for the truth, and I said, "Oh, you know what? I'm no good at telling this story. Auntie Almo, would you like to tell it?" I bent down, handed the mic toward my darling great-aunt, and she delivered. With the awesome power of a Worthy Matron of the Eastern Star, she gave it her all, and the crowd went wild.

-1951-

I ran in terror, up the drive with the grass squares, to the front door. Almo ran out of the house and caught me up in her arms. Gurgling gasps escaped my small body out of me, as she scooped me up. Putting me on my feet she held my shoulders, looked me in the eye and said God would protect me every minute of my life. While she told me this, she circled her right hand over my head, held my gaze with magnetic blue eyes, and said, "The Circle of God's love is around you. You have nothing to fear."

An enveloping hug followed, sweet with her rose cologne. She assured me that she was one of God's soldiers, and it was her duty to keep me, her children Marsha and Roger, and Uncle Chuck safe. She was a rock. She took no prisoners in her war on lies. She appreciated a hard-won truth and, if you struggled but still rose to the occasion of facing her and telling it all — you were saved.

When I was in college, had a car, and could drive anywhere I wanted, I'd visit Almo. She and I drank sweet tea in her kitchen and laughed about our ice cream trips and the cowboys. The highlight of this story is that my great-aunt believed that ice cream made life better. She always had it in her freezer, and through the years, we laughed about how she saw it as a gift from heaven.

On our trips, she knew the best place to get it on the steep winding Ridge Route out of Los Angeles to the San Joaquin Valley. Lebec is a little town tucked halfway between, in the Sierra Pelona Mountains. Winter snows close this high pass, frustrating commerce between LA and Sacramento but thrilling my girls and me on our Christmas trips to The Ranch.

Almo told me how wide-eyed I was when we stopped at what she called the Cowboy Café at Grapevine, the end of the Ridge Route on the San Joaquin side of the mountains. It was filled with coffee-drinking, real-looking cowboys. We'd stop for a "rest and refresh," which meant going to the bathroom and washing our hands. The cowboys had their hats off to eat in the café. Their faces were red up to the line where their hats met their sweaty foreheads. They'd pretend to tip their hats to the tall, regal lady and her grandniece. She said I was open-mouthed and agog, face to face with real live cowboys.

When we arrived at The Ranch, the sisters, Almo and my grandmother Edna started laughing, hugging, lifting, kissing, and catching up before we even got into the house. These were my women, fussing over tea and sandwiches, their voices rising and falling like music.

Allowed to roam The Ranch, there were rules. Never go as far as the road, keep your eyes open for rabid jackrabbits, don't go behind the barn, stay away from the outhouse, you might fall in, and don't play with any wild kittens, they bite. Monsters.

In the afternoon, the two sisters chatted in the kitchen, drinking iced tea in the fading light. "We heard a ruckus outside and saw you running as fast as your little feet could run, chased by an angry brood hen."

I must have gone behind the barn. Curious, going further than I should, I wanted to see the monsters for myself.

The sisters saw me through the kitchen window first. I was being chased by an angry hen. Then, they heard my words. As I ran, I circled my head, tears flying and gulping for air, "I am not afraid, I am not afraid, I am not afraid," racing until I hit the door of the back porch. When we met, I was scooped up and double loved, safe in the arms of my women. I told them everything, hiccups, sobs, tears, but I could only choke out, "I circled, I circled."

Together, we went to Sunday services in the Brethren Church in Strathmore. This simple white wooden church surrounded by acres of corn was founded by their father, Jacob W. Mishler. I sat between them and watched every move. When the music started, I stood up with kid-like confidence on the straight-backed wooden pew. I could feel their warm bodies in pretty flowered dresses, safe, while they sang "The Old Rugged Cross" with full-throated joy, louder than anybody.

This was the story loved by so many people who were touched by my great-aunt.

Her headstone reads: *"A Circle of God's Love Is Around You"* Almo *Mishler Myers 1904-2006.*

Six

Who's the Indian?

Who wouldn't believe it? We had proof. I was born with thick, straight, black hair and black eyes, and when my youngest daughter was born with the same, the cry went out! We have another one! Then, when she married and had her babies, the same thing. It was solid. The true story of the Redmonds — my great-grandmother Maud Ellen, grandmother Lalan, grandfather Lester, and mother Ina Mae — was told with grainy pictures and a flourish of old documents.

The story started with this:

Our Redmond ancestor was Black Irish, the result of inbreeding with invaders from the Spanish Armada, which landed on the coast of Ireland in 1588. It gets better. Our ancestor was either a horse thief or he stole a loaf of bread. It all depended on the teller. The man was a criminal or a saint. My family opted for maximum unfair treatment. Because of his illegal behavior, he was indentured as a slave to a fur company operating out of Canada. After he nobly paid off his indenture, he looked for a wife. Since there were no white women available, he married a woman from the Panawahpskek (Penobscot) tribe. Since they were poor, our ancestor and his native wife walked over 200 miles from St. John, New Brunswick, Canada to Maine. There was just enough documented history, letters, maps, and pictures to allow for time travel, skipping three or four generations, added color and shading, to make it absolutely true. This truth was celebrated my entire life. I passed it onto my daughters and told the story to my grandchildren. It got better each time, and kept their attention when I added the day I learned to speak up and stand tall. The day I spent with my great-grandmother, the half-breed Indian Maud Ellen Redmond.

⌒℮⌯

"Do you know how to use the toilet?" Standing at the front door, Maud was tall and wrapped in a multi-colored Indian blanket. Her grey hair hung in a single long braid over her left shoulder, and she looked down at me. I'd been brought in the early dawn by my grandmother Lalan to stay with her mother-in-law. My mother was in Southern California recovering from her third stillbirth.

Maud's two-story ranch house on Eucalyptus Avenue in Lindsay was the house of the notorious Redmond brothers. Horace and Maud Ellen raised their sons Lester Oliver, my grandfather, and Raymond Everett here. My memory is taking very careful steps over crunchy gravel in the pitch-black morning; the only light cast by the car head-lights behind us. The still air was infused by the pungent eucalyptus trees, dry dirt, and grass. Lalan walked me up the front steps, quietly asking me to watch my step and not scuff my shoes.

I stood, quiet, as big as I could, with thumb at the ready, and waited. The porch light flicked on, and the door opened to my great-grandmother. She bent down to look at me eye to eye, and I must have nodded yes to the question of using a toilet. She said goodbye to my grandmother and told me to follow her. She led me in the dim light to a latched door behind the pantry on the back porch. The latch was high so she unlatched it and put a rock between it and the door frame to keep it ajar for me. She was satisfied. "We're going to tell stories while the sun comes up." She ushered me onto the staircase.

As I looked up, the dark wooden stairs looked like forever. It was fascinating — the walls were lined with pictures of stern-looking people, hanging rugs, and dead animal heads. As we climbed, one big stretch step at a time, she said, looking down at me, "Hey little girl, I have some pretty good stories about what's on that wall."

The dead faces and bared teeth looked down at me, and I shivered.

When we reached the top of the stairs, she instructed me to "turn right." I hesitated, and Maud taught me right and left. In fact, she repeated the lesson often, in every way imaginable that day. On the second story landing, I saw the stairs going up to another floor. I was not just curious, I was motivated to explore. She urged me forward to the room where she wanted us to read, and the tallest woman I'd ever seen walked in from the left. My eyes must have gotten huge, and Maud must have felt me stall. She said, "That's Sally, my friend. Say hello to her."

I squeaked "Hello," and Maud knelt down beside me and moved her long grey braid to the other side of her deeply wrinkled, dark-skinned face. She said simply, "Say it stronger." She stood up, held my shoulders and turned me back to Sally, and instructed me. "Take a breath, think of what you want to say. Now, say it."

I looked up high, directly into Sally's face, she smiled, and I said "Hello!" Sally shook my hand and said something nice, turned, and walked down the stairs. I looked up, and Maud nodded her approval.

She taught me to stand straight and speak out.

∼✑⌇

Maud said she was American Indian. She wore clothing associated with American Indian tribes and had blankets, beads, and animal heads all over her home. She said she was from a tribe in Maine who lived and hunted by the Penobscot River. She gave me a silver and turquoise turtle ring on one visit, and it still sits in my jewelry chest. I believed her with all my heart and soul. I was proud. She showed me strength, asked me to think, and required more of me than any adult in my world. I was a little kid, but in all our visits through the years, she taught me what I needed to learn.

-2013-

When it became available, my daughter and I took DNA tests, excited to confirm our family's exotic heritage. Then I got a call from my dark-haired daughter. "Mom! I'm white! I'm 98.9% white! Who's the Indian?" I tried to think back through the web of stories and could only say . . . I'm sorry! It must be wrong! When I got my DNA, it mapped English, Irish, French, and German. It skipped Penobscot and found France. What the hell? I had to get to the bottom of this.

I asked my aunt Joanne, the widow of my mom's brother Everett, Maud's grandson, and the only living adult left, about this conundrum, and she replied with an enthusiastic laugh, "Ha! She lied. She lied about it all her life after Horace died. She was crazy." Why a vivid lie told as truth for generations?

I think she was fascinated with the idea and all she had to do was look in the mirror. She had the look, so why not assume the character? What did Maud Ellen Redmond have to lose, her reputation? What else is there to do on a huge olive ranch, in a big old dark house, your husband dead, and heads on the staircase grinning down at you?

Lalan picked me up at the end of that day with Maud, and we went to her single-story, white-washed house on Westwood Avenue. It had a neat walkway leading to a porch with trailing roses on both sides of the porch. The smell of lilacs and cake perfumed the walk leading to the front door.

Lalan was delicate, small, gentle, and gossip was magically turned into mist when she was around. She never ever had a bad word for anybody. This remarkable woman with the lyrical name, Lalan Layde Anthony-Redmond, saved "pennies and bills" every day of her life. From the day she and her four sisters stepped off the train from Tennessee and planted their tiny feet in California, she saved. By the time she married Lester and added the marriage gift from her father and mother-in-law, Horace and Maud Ellen Redmond, she had enough to walk into a bank and buy a house in her name. It wasn't the pride of ownership; it was the quiet determination to provide.

Cake and coffee with sweet cream in flowered cups and pretty dishes was a must for the people she loved. She swayed around the kitchen, singing the changed lyrics to one of my favorite songs. *"Oh, I knew you were coming, so I baked a cake, baked a cake, baked a cake. Oh, I knew you were coming, so I baked a cake, How-ja-do, How-ja-do, How-ja-do."*

This song and dance was ours, me on the seat of a wooden chair with chocolate on my face and her pretty voice swirling around the steam of perking coffee. Cake was part of being with her, a different flavor, in the middle of the dining room table at every visit, no matter where the table sat or how big or small the table was. She believed that cake under a glass-domed top showed love.

The "notorious" son of Maud and Horace, my grandfather Lester Redmond settled me in his lap while he smoked his pipe and told stories of the black Irish, dangerous ocean voyages, our slave ancestor, the fur trade, and the life of Indian ladies along the Penobscot River. He'd laugh, and in his exaggerated Maine accent, describe winters in Bangor, Maine. "Ayuh, it was cold enough to freeze your nose hai-ah (hair)," then show me, tipping his head back to let me look up his nose. His voice and our laughter are as clear in my mind as if I'd seen him last weekend.

After he died, Lalan moved to Van Nuys, a suburb of Los Angeles, closer to Mom's brother Everett and his growing family and to us.

Seven

The Complexity of Plaid

"Life is like a bicycle. To keep your balance
you must keep moving."
– *Albert Einstein*

I was nearly five when Nancy arrived, and when she did, she was my prize. Nancy, the bright red bicycle with extra wheels on the back, brought a whole new dimension to my world. We'd moved to a bigger house with two bedrooms on Dixey Drive in San Dimas. I had a bedroom of my own and found a way to sneak Picket in to sleep on my bed.

Dad adjusted Nancy so I could throw everything I had into my ride. The driveway was paved, not dirt, and seemed infinite. I told Picket we would play 1-2-3-go! I furiously peddled back and forth for hours. Picket barked and acted crazy while I laughed and squealed with delight. Picket chased cars and wore down the grass from the side of the house, all the way to the driveway. I rode behind him and said we were soldiers. He hated the fence, and so did I. We wanted the freedom of vast spaces. No, we wanted the street!

One morning, Picket and I awoke to a lady — not my mother, cooking bacon and eggs in our kitchen. I recognized her as our next-door neighbor . . . one of the Holy Rollers. At that age, I knew to be polite and quiet, and I knew right and wrong. But my mother's criticism of their religious practice was convincing. "Filled with the spirit of Jesus, they cry out and speak in tongues." She added, "For heaven's sake," sounding superior, "at least we Presbyterians are quiet." Dad complained about the number of cars parked in front of our fence on the nights people gathered to worship at their house. Picket acted as if they were dangerous intruders. I was on the side of my family.

Five in two months, already learning to be brave and loyal, I thought about the strength Maud taught me, so I listened carefully as she made my breakfast. She was too nice to be on the wrong side, and I struggled not to like her.

"Do you know the Lord takes a baby when he knows it's time?" I was stumped. "Shall we pray for its soul, you and I?" Her voice rose with her arms, and she started to sway and say a loud sounding prayer. I squeezed my eyes shut. I thought I knew what she was praying about, and it scared me. I said "amen" at the right time. The eggs were tough, the toast was too toasty and still had the crust, and there were no apple semi-circles or jam. But I knew better than to say anything.

Before I choked down the last of the crust, my father drove up. When he came into the house, he told me he was driving me to The Ranch to stay with my grandparents, Edna and Earl Shryer. He thanked the next-door neighbor for her help and for making breakfast. I stood behind Dad, peeked around his legs, and watched her leave. I stood tall, and in the voice Maud taught me, said, "Thank you."

Mom said they were "A little nutty if you ask me." I thought I knew what she was talking about after the loud prayer the neighbor had called on us to pray, but let it go. I liked her.

It dawned on me that this trip was going to be fun, and I forgot to be worried about Mom not being there and the Holy Roller making my breakfast. I was getting used to being moved around, and as long as I could take Nancy and Picket to The Ranch, all was good. We packed my clothes for a fun trip and made sure we had plenty of snacks and biscuits for Picket and me. Nothing could go wrong.

We drove for hours through Los Angeles, up the Ridge Route, and stopped at Lebec for ice cream and "refreshing"; the bathroom for us and for Picket, a tree. Dad let me check Nancy with pretend precision before we got back in the car. "I checked the wheels and the chain. She looks secure." He put his fingers in his lips and whistled for Picket. We were satisfied that everything was ship-shape and took off on our trip.

Dad loved to sing songs, so in his deep baritone, he entertained me.

In Dublin's fair city,
where the girls are so pretty
I first set my eyes on sweet Molly Malone.
As she wheeled her wheelbarrow
through streets broad and narrow,
Crying cockles and mussels alive a-live O!

A-live a-live O! A-live a-live O!
A-live a-live O! A-live a-live O!
Crying cockles and mussels alive a-live O!

When we arrived at The Ranch, I saw the old sidewalk as a race track for the very first time. From the front gate, it wound around the house and straight out to the back and ended just before the huge gravel driveway and the barn. We could turn left and fly back to the beginning. We're finally free! No fence and no chickens will dare get in our way!

My grandfather Earl swept up any grass and twigs, making it safe for me and my bicycle. He laughed when I demonstrated my speedy skills and said, "By golly, I think she may not need those extra wheels for long." I felt proud.

∼℮∽

In a picture, I can see how my loyalty showed in my uniform. In the photo, I'm a little girl standing on the bumper of an old truck. My grandfather is standing next to me. We're wearing shirts tucked in, denim pants with the cuffs turned up, and our hands are tucked into our pants pockets. We're serious, looking into the camera, Picket in front, none of us smiling.

My father told me his version of this story with heart-wrenching emotion over coffee many years later after he sold The Ranch. "Grand-dad and I watched you ride. I was so proud of you." He told me how his father locked eyes with him at that moment and nodded. Grandfather was there, he would care, and he would protect me, the surviving child.

ৎৎৎ

Mom was in bed when we got home, so it was up to Dad to dress and care for me. She was happy to see me and let me crawl up on her bed so she could hear all my exciting stories about my adventures with Nancy, Picket, my grandpa and grandma, and The Ranch. My grandfather had taken the back wheels off the bike and gave me the first lesson on two wheels. Before we drove away, Grandpa told my dad, "Make sure she gets it down. She's a brave one."

I wanted my mom to hear everything. I was pretty excited, hopeful, and felt so, so very big. Picket did his crazy dog dance wanting me to play, Nancy was waiting for me, and my mom was bedridden after the hysterectomy after the fourth stillbirth. She said, "They took care of it." The doctors could not explain why our babies died before or just after they were born.

I wasn't five and wouldn't start school until after summer, so the childcare solution that spring was taking me to the elementary school where he taught 6th grade. He was going to put me in the kindergarten class, in a real school. I was thrilled.

Mom had the energy to tell him which dress to get out for me, where the shoe polish was, and what to make for my lunch. My father bragged about "spit and polish" from his time in the army and used his skills to "get'er done, soldier." He used the southern hill country accent he learned from his army buddy. Silly Picket sniffed and sneezed, and we, using army precision, made sure all my shoes were shiny and clean. Then, he had to iron my clothes. How much cussing could one little kid hear? I'd cover my ears and run to Mom. She'd yell, "Darn it, Loren — stop cussing in front of her!"

Getting ready for school was painful. My father couldn't tie ponytails or fix braids, and when he tried, he'd cuss. He'd get frustrated with what to say and sputter words like "cheese," "stinky dog dang," then he'd give up and yell "shit." My mother laughed and complained about her stitches. She had me bring the brush and rubber bands to her. Sitting on the bed, she gently brushed my hair and hummed — a welcome relief from the multi-thumbed cuss machine.

He didn't call the school to ask if I could stay in the afternoon kindergarten class, he just took me with him. No one could say no to this tall man with a cute little girl in a plaid taffeta dress, white socks, and spit-polished saddle shoes.

In the classroom, it was nap time, and I went down on brown craft paper. *Who takes a nap on paper?* I'd never seen that before. It was unsettling. I didn't know to bring a blanket. I wished for mine and made a plan to tell Mom. But I fell asleep as all good nappers do.

I heard the teacher say, "Now, children, keep your eyes closed. When I call the color you're wearing, you can open your eyes and get up."

No problem — I knew my colors and numbers. She called a color, one by one:

"Red" — "Green" — "Yellow" — "Blue?"

I started to panic — I had all those colors in my dress. Which one should I choose? I didn't know what to do. My confidence ebbed as worry took over.

I scrunched and covered my eyes with my hands. As the teacher went through every color she could think of, getting a little louder, then with some frustration, she paused, took a deep breath, and finally said, "Plaid!" I jumped up. I saw the children standing around me, laughing and pointing at me. I was embarrassed, standing small in my taffeta plaid dress with a starched navy blue petticoat.

According to his tale, when he came to get me, Dad said my little soul was crushed, and he wanted to make it better. His solution was ice cream. It worked. We sat on high-backed chairs at the drug store counter in San Dimas, ordered hot fudge sundaes, and talked about school, other kids, and the complexity of plaid. I rose from the taffeta crumple of my first day in a real school.

While we were out, my sweet mother carefully moved out of bed and made square cream cheese and jam sandwiches with the crust cut off, apple semi-circles, and carrot sticks for my triumphant return from school. When I walked in the door, I saw my little table, lunch on a doily with a cloth napkin — just perfect. Picket was allowed to lay on the floor next to my chair while I told him everything about my plaid day.

My mom lost four babies and her grief was replaced by industrious zeal. We marched forward into the wobbly new world with an expanse of exciting unknowns. In the moments between stories and instructions, corrections and baths, tickles and hugs, my life was full. With no other child in the family to create a sharply defined alternate reality, it was up to me to be ready, set to go, paddling alone, in a pool of strong, smart adults.

Eight

Kittens

"Duck and Cover!" We kindergartners learned to prepare for the threat. The Soviet Union could drop an atom bomb on our school at any moment. Lucky for us, we could protect ourselves by diving under our wooden desks and wrapping our arms around our tucked heads. We loved how important it was for our school and the flag that hung in our classroom.

All schoolchildren in the '50s were taught that the Soviet Union was ready to bomb us. We were brave, all nine of us in the kindergarten class at La Verne Heights School. At recess, the monkey bars and swings called us to action, but some of us worried and watched the sky. We thought we were prepared to meet the threat. I did carry the yearning for justice and fair play throughout my young life, but in kindergarten, my primary worry was getting caught sucking my thumb.

I didn't talk about the Soviet threat when Mom and I discussed books and words after school. The added complication of dying from a Soviet bomb simply slipped my mind until we had another drill. I was too young to pull it all together.

According to my mom, our street Dixie Drive was "straight out of a Steinbeck novel." At the time, I was too young to know what she meant, but when I was old enough to read the book, I understood her chilling reference. In the novel, migrants shuffled from one dirty, broken-down roadside camp to another. What I read was the profound evil of class distinction.

Living on our street were all kinds of "riffraff" — her word for our neighbors. The street's surface was almost all dirt and gravel with patches of broken blacktop, and there were a few homes with discarded old cars in the yard. The rusty junk at our house was left behind by the "riffraff" who rented before us. Two old refrigerators and the shell of a broken, wheel-less motorcycle sat among the tall weeds and piles of rotting wood in our backyard. The mess provided a country for packs of rats. Picket knew his job and did his best to take out the rats, but it was too much for my mother. She put her foot down with volume. "Damn it, Loren, clean up the godforsaken junk!"

We were the high-class, soon to move up, renters.

Family weekend time became cutting and hauling. With the yard clean, we put up a clothesline and brought out the folding chairs. We could sit in our de-junked dirt yard, dream of better things to come, and drink iced tea while Picket perked his ears for rats.

My mother regularly reinforced the idea of status. We were better than this. We certainly didn't deserve this poverty, and specifically, she didn't. Our neighbors deserved our pity because they were less fortunate than us. This class-based bias was lost on me at the time because I lived in a vivid landscape of love, playful friends, dirt, and dogs.

The Holy Rollers next door were a noisy group with lots of friends. I always said hello to the nice lady that made tough eggs. I loved the Mexican kids in the apartment across the street. We rode our bikes together, covered in sugar, sweat, and dirt, acting goofy.

The next house up the street had a "family."

We were never allowed to play with the sad-eyed seven or eight-year-old girl, though I wanted to. She watched us with blank staring eyes. A slight smile awakened on her face when we called out to her. We rode our bikes close to the bushes and hid as we spied on the house. Maybe we could get her to talk and give up her secrets.

One day, she put her hand up to the fence.

Braking hard, I slowly rode over to her. The other kids stopped on the other side of the street and watched. The girl and I touched, hand to hand, eye to eye, wordless together. In seconds a man burst out of the house, screaming curses at her to get away from the fence. He was a black-haired running monster spitting words and wearing big boots. His eyes flashed in fury as his long hair flew in the breeze.

She smiled at me and turned to go. He grabbed her arm and struck her head as they walked to the house.

All mothers agreed. None of us were allowed to play with the girl from that family. We wondered why, but unable to conceive of any reason short of disease, we went along with our spy plan to draw her out anyway. One day, I casually asked my mom about the family. She whipped around, held my arm, bent down, and said, "Young lady! You are never, ever, allowed to go near that family. Do you hear me?"

I stammered, "But the girl."

She was steadfast in her warning.

Together, the girl and I defied the warnings of my mother and the threats of her father. We secretly met and shared my packets of Jell-O. We sat in the bushes, quiet together, licking the sweet sugar off our fingers. We grinned, showing our green and yellow teeth, sharing whispered dreams of two bikes and endless streets. We wished for ice cream sundaes and banana splits. Hidden, we smiled and touched fingers and foreheads, through the chain link, friends forever.

Mom, Dad, and I said prayers every night, and, in the end, I asked Jesus to protect every single family member, my dog Picket, my friends, and the girl behind the fence.

I had a few questions about the words, but I kept them to myself.

> *Now I lay me down to sleep.*
> *I pray the Lord, my soul, to keep.*
> *If I should die before I wake.*
> *I pray the Lord, my soul, to take.*

What if I fall asleep before I pray?
Will God remember me if I forget to pray?
Who will take me if I die?
Who will tell you?
Will you miss me?

∾୧ଡ଼୨

That summer between kindergarten and first grade, my parents camped in Canada. Being too young to camp, I was dropped off at The Ranch, the summer drop-off point for Picket, Nancy, and me.

My beloved Shryer grandparents, Earl and Edna, oranges, figs, animals, and chores awaited our chaotic trio. I loved gathering eggs and taking fruit and vegetable scraps to the pig behind the barn. Picket could sneak up the stairs to snuggle in the cozy brass bed. Earl let me sit on his lap to read the evening paper while grandmother sang hymns as she cleaned up after dinner. I showed them my pledge of allegiance, and they clapped. They were proud of me. Wrapped in love, I didn't worry about the Soviets and atom bombs. The Holy Rollers, my friends on the street, all the animals on the ranch, wild and tame, even the family on the other side of the fence were protected by my nightly prayers.

The wild animal policy was regularly reinforced on The Ranch. "Don't touch." They can bite and "don't get attached," you may never see them again. I understood life was wild and short, but one day I found something. It was a feral cat who had her kittens on an old blanket in a dark, dusty corner of the barn. She hissed at me when I came within a couple of feet of her. I instantly broke the second rule and got attached. She was beautiful, white, and grey. Her five cute kittens were all different colors, even an orange and white one, my favorite.

I saw how she wanted to protect her little family, so I got other pieces of blankets from an old wooden box under a dusty workbench. They didn't smell like gasoline or oil, so they were safe for her. She let me get close enough to move the pieces into a bigger barrier to keep the kittens safe. Foxes had gotten into the chicken coop and killed some of the hens as they slept on their eggs. It wasn't a great find during the egg collection chore, and I prayed foxes didn't kill kittens.

I brought her clean, cool water to drink. If I gave my grandmother Edna a compelling story, she'd warm up some cream for me to take to the mother. After a while, the cat let me close, girl face to fuzzy face, and finally, she licked my hand.

Edna knew what I was up to and didn't really approve of feeding the wild cats in the barn. They had a job. They were allowed to live because they caught mice and other small rodents. They were not pets — ever. The cat and I sat together a little bit each day until the cute little kittens opened their eyes. I prayed they'd be quiet. They weren't.

One morning I went to check, and they were gone. The space was empty. I walked around the barn and heard the cat yowling as if she was crying. I stood still, and she moved carefully around the corner and looked at me — her only friend. Then she turned and disappeared into the orange trees.

When my grandfather came in from the groves, I asked. He told me he found them and drowned the kittens in a gunny sack. My world tilted. Kittens and puppies were a source of joy. They lived and went to families, or at least they were named so they could get into heaven. It was simple, a truth, a routine, a reality. My kid question, "WHY?" resulted in him telling me drowning was the most painless way to kill puppies and kittens. The necessity of population control left me with no counterargument. I disagreed. I was helpless. I felt something besides sadness, like a little door closing.

It was only after I decided to ensure every kitten was named out loud that I took off my slippers, knelt on the round braided rug, and started to pray. The windows were open to the light of the full moon and the sweet, Central California breeze. It floated through the screen with a hint of orange blossom as I wept and said the prayer for the poor drowned kittens — *"If they should die before they wake, I pray the Lord their souls to take."* I didn't really care about my soul.

Was it my fault? I felt guilt over the kittens. At that time of life, I'd learned that naming doomed animals and insects could get them into heaven. It was simple in the beginning, but I began to feel uncertain about the timing between being killed and being named. I justified any difficulty the kittens might have had, nameless in heaven, with my ignorance of their murder. The burden was outrageous for a small girl. I began to think my responsibility might be hard. How was I going to do what needed to be done?

Nine

Friends for Lunch

I sang "I'm a Little Bird of Blue" in the La Verne Heights School Fall Show. The note in my baby book reads, "She was very good!" My parents showered me with praise and took me out for banana splits at Betsy Ross. I had the strong confidence of a well-appreciated six-year-old girl. Weirdly, I told my mother to skip my birthday party. I'm quoted, "I don't want a party, just cake." I was good in my world, "she's pretty domineering," but "so far so good" . . . so says the book. The picture is of a non-smiling, sullen me and a group of happy little friends.

∾

That summer, Picket, Nancy the red bike, and I took our yearly trip to The Ranch while my parents vacationed in Mexico. I was on my way to second grade, and I had confidence. My universe of chores, learning to ride Honey Boy the golden palomino, feeding the chickens, collecting eggs, and making up stories filled my days. I looked forward to fried chicken, Jell-O salads, white bread, and freshly made butter . . . and singing hymns.

One bright hot day, I was walking back from reading in the cool shade of the chicken coop when my grandfather Earl called out to me.

"It's your job to catch the chicken today," he said. The tall, straight as a steel rod, no-nonsense grandpa handed me a hen catcher. The hen catcher was a thin pole with a deadly loop of wire on one end and a pull gadget on the handle. The loop caught a chicken's foot as she walked over the wire, invisible on the ground, hidden by sweet grain.

"Everyone needs to know how to catch and kill a chicken," he said with ultimate certainty like a universal rule. He believed the earlier you learned the ways of the farm, the better, stronger, and tougher you became. He saw this heartless task as character building for the girl, not a boy. But, I was not convinced. Not really on board. We dressed alike; I tried to walk, talk, and not cry like him. I tried hard to be like him.

My heart was cloaked in dread. The chickens grouped around me like girlfriends as I sprinkled grain in their pen. When I wanted a quiet place to read, I took my book into the cool brooding hutch and kept the door open. We were snug, the air warmed by the summer sun. Hens came in slowly, and some settled in next to me, and some flapped up to the top nests to watch. They would cluck quietly and peck at my shirt lovingly while I read about faraway lands. I named all the animals on the farm but I named the hens with numbers and kept track of each one because so many of them landed on the dinner table. I wrote descriptions in a little book my grandfather gave to me to make notes about each hen. "Number One — white with yellow feathers on one wing." "Number Three — one fluffy black foot." Each one was painstakingly identified. I tried to be as neat as he was when he wrote in his irrigation book.

When it was time to pick, it tore at my soul to be the one to choose. Praying as I reached for the latch on the gate into the hen yard, my grandfather said, "Now, when you get in, close the gate. Put the loop on the ground. When a hen steps in, pull the lever and catch her foot."

The instructions were to catch and kill — my heart was in my throat as I prayed, "Please, please, Jesus, please make the chickens run away from me." But the hens knew me. My voice was music to them. I was the one who brought special grain and gently petted them when I gathered eggs. They clucked sweetly when I put my hand under their warm bodies. They trusted me with their lives.

The hens came slowly toward me, then they turned and ran around. They eyed me with attachment, maybe catching the narcotic aroma of grain on my jeans, and recognized I was safe. Number Two stepped into the loop. I did what I was told and pulled the lever. I cried as the sweet hen flapped her wings and struggled, but I was caught in an impossible chain of events and could not let her go.

My grandfather whooped and grabbed the chicken by her delicate little feet. He lifted her into the air on the way to the stump and the ax. Number Two was for lunch, and there was nothing I could do to save her. I wiped my tears so my grandfather would skip the lecture about boys and crying on a farm.

I was conflicted at an early age. I learned about sudden, gruesome death on our hill of gophers, but we didn't have squished gophers for lunch. I treasured every kitten born to our cats and mourned the passing of every pet, but we didn't eat them. The gopher bodies got the dump, the kittens and birds got a funeral. At The Ranch, a rooster made a great soup, the cow became hamburger, the horses turned into who knows what, and my hilarious friend, the pig, became a lot of things, not the least of which was bacon. Becoming friends with the chickens was silly, but the hens were perfect sisters for the last surviving girl. I hung on to my pledge to save as many as I could. My grandfather didn't think it was good for me to be friends with every horse, bug, and caterpillar. He had a point. It was a very big job to name the doomed.

My grandparents decided to up the game. My grandmother showed me what happens when you don't have an ax and a stump. She named this show, "Here's how we do it in Kansas." It sounds simple and harmless. What's so bad about Kansas? I was about to find out they were monsters of a whole different breed. To this day, someone says, "Kansas," and my mind halts as the nanoseconds tick by, and I remember I'm a rational adult.

My grandmother appeared holding a chicken by the feet while I sat astride my kid saddle on two sawhorses. She had Number Nine, and the hen was frantic. I closed my eyes and prayed for her soul. I thought about leaping off my pretend horse, tripping Grandmother, and rescuing my friend. But that option was way out of line and just the imaginary conviction of a confident girl.

I watched my grandmother explain how all her sisters had to learn this way of killing a chicken. Sitting on my saddle, a light, gentle summer breeze ruffled my ponytail tied in a red scarf; the sun sparkled in the blue sky as my grandmother took the chicken by the neck and twisted . . . hard. I was stunned into silence.

I watched Number Nine squawk then gurgle as she passed out. My hands flew to my face, and I started to cry. My grandmother put the hen's head under a plank, stood with one foot on each end. Holding Nine's feet, she pulled up with all her might. The chicken's carcass was headless and spurted blood as my grandmother let her go. Her headless body ran in random directions, flinging warm blood on my saddle, my legs, and my boots. I started to scream.

I fainted, they said, and fell off my saddle. I woke up in my bed with my grandparents looking at me. "Come, dear. Let's have some orange juice, and then we can read a bible story." My Earl and Edna looked at each other with resignation and nodded in silent agreement. I'm sure this is the time they decided I needed to be toughened. Not a boy, but it's all we have . . .

Without my knowledge and apparently in agreement with my father, the plan was to teach me what I needed to know about living on a farm. It was brutal and tough. I can't imagine my mother being good with this.

We came home from Sunday services, and thankfully, for supper, we had meatloaf.

Ten

Mud Pies

"**W**e won't talk. *They can tie us to the monkey bars, and we won't talk.*" This is the clarion sound of the playground stand; when we're invaded, we will be strong. Duck and Cover.

Our creative imagination could be crushed by any rational adult, but lucky for us our teacher overheard our talk and decided to use our fervor as a teachable moment. We were called into the classroom at the end of recess.

She asked what was on our minds. We spun our concerns into a fantastic web, tumbling over each other like playful bear cubs, as we slowly learned to share and take turns. Our teacher asked questions, and we answered, raising hands with energy. Then . . . she asked, "Would you like to design your own pledge on paper and sign it?" The thrill!

The lessons wove second grade kid logic, art, history, and English into our creation. It took a week to create, and when it was done, we pinned it to the wall. We, students of civic pride, stood in front of the masterpiece designed of our advanced thinking, confident and feeling a little power. Our teacher left us for a minute and returned with the principal. The principal asked us to explain. We clamored to be heard as our teacher gently managed our messy sharing.

"Your country would be proud of you."

Our teacher and the principal clapped. We were taken seriously, and I know it changed a few molecules in each and every one of us.

Her lesson the next day was the duty of voting. It was our job to learn as much as we could about our nation, and when we turned 21, we could cast our vote — another shift, in reality, my heart beat to a new and exciting drum. We had faith in ourselves — however young the beautiful pride, however fragile the confidence, we were wrapped up in faith . . . it sounded like the kind of faith my grandparents talked about.

⁓

I loved to put on tea parties in the barn at The Ranch, and I eagerly planned the next one. My grandparents, Earl and Edna, did what I asked to make it nice. Grandfather set up hay bales in the barn, so whoever needed a seat for the tea party had one. There was even a bale for the table. My grandmother made a tablecloth and tea napkins from soft, faded, flour sackcloth. She gave me stitching lessons while adding pink and blue rick-rack to the edges. Snug in her rocking chair and me on the footstool, we sang the song while we sewed and talked about Jesus.

> *I come to the garden alone, while the dew is still on the roses,*
> *And the voice I hear, falling on my ear,*
> *The Son of God discloses.*
>
> *And He walks with me, and He talks with me,*
> *And He tells me I am His own,*
> *And the joy we share as we tarry there,*
> *None other has ever known.*

Jesus, whom I believed with all my heart and soul was a real person, had not shown up at any party so far. All the adults I knew had come and had a really good time. But, not Jesus. I thought it was because I wasn't old enough, or not "faithing" enough, or something. I had to figure out a way to meet. If I followed all the steps in the song my grandmother and I sang while she cooked or rocked in her chair crocheting, it could work. I was the only one who couldn't see Him. Maybe this time, if I followed all the instructions, He would appear, and we could talk.

> *And He walks with me, and He talks with me,*
> *And He tells me I am His own . . .*

I wrote tea party invitations on notepaper my grandmother gave to me. All my friends, Honey Boy, the nosey golden palomino in his stable, maybe Jesus, Picket with his party scarf, and hopefully a stray chicken would come. I'd bring some good seed in my pocket just in case I had to lead a shy hen to the party.

I resolved to follow the song. Maybe it would be the answer.

The really good stuff for the mud pies was in the garden. But, the garden was terrifying and lay in wait for me. It was filled with jumping spiders, creepy slugs, wasp nests, gooey snails, and the torn-up body parts of whatever animal the cats killed.

At the kitchen table and at the big dining room table, Edna set a place for Jesus. These grandparents said the meal prayer as if He was sitting there. When I asked why I couldn't see Him, the answer was, "it required faith." When I had enough of it, I'd see Him.

The plan began in earnest. I had a few questions for Him and a party planned. I had to wake up in the dark, get dressed, get out quietly and be in the garden before sunrise. The night before, I laid out my clothes and planned my route, plotting each step to avoid the staircase's squeaky parts and the sticking door on the back porch. I had to do this alone; the instructions were clear.

> *I come to the garden alone, while the dew is still on the roses,*
> *And the voice I hear, falling on my ear,*
> *The Son of God discloses.*

I needed enough "faith" for it to work. My grandmother told me "faith" came with strength. I hoped I could get enough strength from praying so my faith could be heard and he would come. I fell asleep repeating my prayer, "Please God give me 'faith.' I'm strong enough now, please, please, so I can hear the voice falling on me, please."

I woke up in the dark, got dressed, and tiptoed down the stairs, across the back porch, down the back steps, across the grass; I stood at the edge of the lawn looking into the garden for a safe path. The garden was guarded by a tall scraggly scarecrow. He was staring, waiting for me. Taking a deep breath and saying a quick "faith" prayer, I shuddered and took the first step. Watching for slugs, dead rodent parts, and jumping spiders, I picked my spot to wait.

> *. . . to the garden alone while the dew is still on the roses.*

I stood still. The leaves on the big fig tree rustled in the cool, light, pre-dawn breeze. An owl, perched on the farmhouse roof, softly hooted. The smell of rich dirt mixed with the faint perfume of horse manure and the pale scent of roses. I prayed there was enough dew, and it stayed on the roses long enough for it to happen. I knew in my heart if I did this right, He would show up, and we could "tarry" and talk. I knew He would be kind and understanding. We had to talk, face to face — the party, the place at the table, did He know me, and did He hear me when I prayed?

I waited.

On The Ranch, dawn started when the sun rose over the Sierra Nevada Mountains in the East, then it peeked over the top of the barn. Breathing quietly, I noticed the sky changing just a bit. The morning was cool. I held my breath — I was alone in the garden, there was dew everywhere — even on the spider webs, which of course I watched very closely. I kept "faithing" and breathing.

I waited . . . and waited . . . and waited . . . and waited.

Nothing happened.

It got warmer and lighter, and the dew started to steam off the leaves and flowers. I began to wonder if I missed Him. *"Did He come, and I didn't see Him?"* *"Oh no, did he walk by when I was looking at the spiders?"* My breath quickened.

The loud voice of my grandmother called out of the kitchen window overlooking the lawn to the garden, "What in the world are you doing out there? Come in for breakfast right now and wipe your feet."

I walked out of the garden, head down, not caring about slugs or spiders, up the steps to the house, and opened the squeaky door. I wiped my feet and shuffled through the kitchen to the dining room. My grandfather was in from the orchards. My humming grandmother fussed over the dining room table. Right there at the end, I saw the empty chair for Jesus. My "faithing" a failure, I slowly entered to plates of toast, bacon, fried eggs, and glasses filled with freshly squeezed orange juice. I slumped into my chair, head down, and heard my grandmother say in a voice loud enough to be heard over the muffled preaching on the radio, "What in the dickens has gotten into you?" Walking into the dining room, wiping her hands on a dish towel she looked at me.

I stayed silent. I looked at my grandfather out of the corner of my eye and got a glance that meant "get it out and get it out now."

I took a deep breath and said with a shaking voice, "He never came," and tried really hard not to cry. A bomb could have gone off, and they wouldn't have heard it. Four eyes were on me waiting . . .

"I got up early enough to be in the garden while the dew was still on the roses," I sobbed, "and He didn't come to tarry with me."

My grandmother made a funny noise, put her hands over her face, and wiped tears from her eyes as she chuckled. My tall, strong grandfather pulled his chair back, got up, picked me up into his arms, and held me while I cried.

Over his shoulder, I looked at Jesus' place and knew He would never come.

Eleven

A Christmas Gang

We — Mom, Dad, and I — went to The Ranch for Christmas, where we joined my aunt Thelma Eugenia, her husband Frank, and their new adopted toddler, Christina. My father's sister and her family lived in Northern California.

Out before dawn for chores, I watched Bach in the chicken run on the way to the barn. The brilliantly plumed rooster stretched his scrawny feathered neck and released his morning aria. Reaching a zenith, he shook his fluffy shoulders and looked around to see if anyone was listening. The hens pecked and clucked and sleepily placed one foot in front of the other, filed out of the hen house, and ignored him.

In winter, the water in the mossy wooden horse trough on the side of the barn froze into a solid plank. My early morning chore was to break up the ice with a small ax I carried in my tool belt. The sun sparkled frost on the barn roof like rhinestones as Honey Boy, the golden palomino, arrived to drink, snorting steam with his hot breath.

My second chore after gathering eggs was to pick oranges for juice. The ancient gathering bag was stiff on my back and too big for my girl body. I forgot to notice anything but the thin layers of frozen puddles of irrigation water that waited for destructive stomps in the freezing shadows of the orange grove. I happily crunched down the row of trees, trying to break up every patch I could find. My mind wandered to breakfast, and my stomach growled.

I turned right and headed for my favorite orange trees to collect oranges for juice. As I turned, I came face to face with three dogs. They weren't familiar, and they stared at me, startled. I knew not to run, so I walked with my eyes down and turned right at the next row. They followed me, and though they kept their distance, I could hear their breath. My heart started to beat fast as I plotted my path, moving slowly, closer to the trees near the house. I weighed the importance of my chore against the necessity of escaping the dogs. It seemed to me that if I sent up a prayer and went about collecting quietly, maybe God or the mythical Jesus would protect me.

I stopped at a tree and started picking. Placing one cold orange at a time in the bag, I could barely manage my shaking hands. I dropped an orange on the ground and froze. It rolled toward the dogs. They stopped. They saw it. I looked at them, cataloging their characteristics. The skinny black one was the leader. The other two were brown, one missing an eye, and the other had open patches of skin and a chewed-off ear. They looked at me. I turned and kept picking. I walked to the second tree. I heard a growl, close, oh so close. I closed my eyes and prayed for girl strength. I turned back to the tree, put the last oranges in my bag, and slowly walked toward the house.

It took every bit of energy to stay slow and not run screaming up the steps. The bag of oranges was heavy, and the stress was big, my heaving breath plume mixed with the sweat on my face in the frosty morning. I reached the porch steps and pulled the bag off my shoulders as the eyes of the ragged dogs bored into my back. Very slowly, I turned to look at them. They were silent, standing on the sidewalk to the house, just looking at me. I'll never know what crazy death wish entered my brain, but I sat down on the step and looked back at them. Very quietly, with a prayer on my lips, I called for them, adding a tiny click of my tongue at the end. The dogs looked at me, and then the black one moved forward and warily walked over to the step. He sniffed my shoes — getting a good whiff of the horse, snorted, looked me in the eye, then turned and ran across the lawn into the grove, followed by his scrawny pack.

I took a deep breath and considered my luck as I gathered my heavy bag of oranges and walked to the porch door. When I turned the handle and walked in, the smells of breakfast fell over me like a blanket. The bright, happy voices of my people rang in the house, and the smell of sweet rolls filled my lungs. As I took off my shoes, my grandfather came out on the back porch to greet me. "I see you got a big bag this morning," he chuckled. "I forgot to warn you to keep your eyes open. There's a mean pack of wild dogs running hereabouts. Did you see anything?"

I said, wanting to keep things even, "Just poor old Bach and Honey Boy."

I was covered in hugs as I walked through the kitchen. My grandfather used the large juice press, and I got the first glass. The portrait of Jesus hung over the breakfast table, his eyes looked toward us, watching.

The juice was cold, tangy, and sweet.

Twelve

Tiny Dancer

"You will be a tall and lovely dancer, my dear." My mother reassured me, the tallest kid with the biggest teeth of all the ballerina butterflies in the recital. She prepared me for being tall with lots of reassuring comments. "It's better to be tall." "It's much easier to carry weight if you're tall." "Don't worry, you'll grow into your teeth."

I was worried.

I wanted to be in toe-shoes by Christmas to participate as a real ballerina in the Christmas recital. I stretched my feet over my back, touching my toes to my forehead. I could do side-to-side splits and split each leg forward. I practiced at home on a rug in my bedroom. I'd stretch and read to Picket, who acted like he cared. I got compliments on my hands, and though my overbite betrayed me during a strong effort, I didn't mind being told to put my front teeth behind my lips. I worked on becoming a dedicated, over-bitten, almost ballerina.

In class on a Wednesday, I stood with the rest of the girls in first-position in our pink leotards and soft, flat ballet shoes, our hands gently positioned in front of our hips, legs in perfect form, waiting for the weekly promotion. As ballet classmates, we supported each other, whispering encouragement to be chosen to be "en pointe."

The teacher walked by, looking us up and down then making eye contact with each student, all of us looked up at her, our hair neat and precise — a group of perfect little girls. She said yes or no to each girl as she came down the line, closer to me. I took a breath and held it. When she got to me, she said, "Please, sweetheart, go sit in the chair over there."

She pointed to the back wall next to the piano. I stopped breathing.

I waited, holding every emotion, looking forward, and heard the other girls either weep with disappointment or squeal with delight. After class dismissal, she came to me and gracefully lowered herself into the seat next to mine. She sighed, looked at me, and said, "Janet, you work very hard, you are a wonderful dancer, and I'm so happy you're in the class. But, you need to tell your mother your feet are not right for "en pointe." Oh no, the dreaded curse of bad feet. "Your tendons are short, and your instep and arch are not high enough for ballet." I think my mouth dropped open, and I know I cried. She patted me on the back as the sound of her voice fogged in my brain as she said, "You know, your feet won't matter in tap dance." Not sweet news for a dancer with ballet dreams.

I tried to stifle my tears with my hands over my face, but the tears flowed through my fingers, out of my control. Collecting my things, I knew I couldn't argue or even ask questions. I was a freak.

I walked to the waiting car of the mother who typically drove me home after class with her daughter, my friend. I struggled to breathe normally and not show emotion on the drive home. The girl didn't say a word as we sat in the back seat together, looking down. She was promoted to toe. Her mother shot "beware" looks through the rearview mirror as we drove home. I needed to give up ballet and practice not caring. I did my best not to care. The least painful way to smooth this over was never to say anything and pretend I was on the way to toe but chose not to. Again, I hoped I'd get away with the lie without crying.

After I gave it some thought, I told my parents I was quitting dance because it was too much and I didn't like it anymore. They were tired from work and didn't seem to care. I was off the hook. Mom yawned and asked a couple of questions, but I didn't tell her about my malformed feet and legs. I said I wanted to play the piano, which I knew she'd go for. She perked up, looking on the sunny side.

Apparently, a daughter with ballerina dreams did not reflect her talent as a mother.

๛

Mom got a job to pay her way through the rest of her degree. She was a secretary, and Dad was teaching junior high. One day a small convertible black Triumph sports car drove up to our house on Dixey Drive and parked on the street in front of the chain-link fence. The driver beeped his horn. I watched through the front window. I saw the driver unwind his tall, large shouldered frame out of the sports car and adjust his sunglasses. My mother was the passenger. I watched, fascinated. She unwound the scarf on her hair, keeping her hair in place, and she smiled at him as she shook out her hair. Dad wasn't home, and, as I walked away from the front window, Picket by my side, I felt uncomfortable. This man was Mr. Stewart, my mom's boss. He was well dressed in a black suit and white shirt. Sometimes he wore just the white shirt, unbuttoned with the sleeves rolled up. He wore black horn-rimmed sunglasses and sported a large, toothy grin as if he'd landed a big deal or a big fish.

Mr. Stewart began to show up with my mother, his beautiful new secretary, after work, every day. She spoke as if it were merely a convenience, nothing to talk about. On one of those days, he asked my mother if he could take me for a drive. My mother clapped and laughed. "Yes!" She was excited for me. I was suspicious. Where was my dad in this?

As we sped down a backcountry street with almost no traffic, me holding on for dear life, he hollered over the whipping wind and the roar of the car, "Your parents are buying a new house in Pomona."

When the car came to a stop, I asked, "How do you know so much about my parents?"

He laughed and gunned the engine. He drove fast, and the rev of the engine seemed to drill down on my worry. As we slowly cruised onto our neighborhood street, Mr. Stewart looked at me and said, "Your neighborhood isn't good enough for your mother." Cold rage simmered on the edge of my mind. As I exited the Triumph, he patted my back like we were friends. Then he said, "Don't worry, kiddo." As he walked to the driver's side, his suit coat slung over his shoulder, he turned and winked. "See you soon, kiddo."

I was definitely not comfortable with this new character in our lives. I was not his kiddo, and I didn't want to see him soon.

That night I heard my parents arguing about moving. Mom claimed that she could no longer live as if they were poor. She needed to live "in a much better house, on a normal street." My father yelled and crashed around because he was being outplayed.

But Mr. Stewart said the same thing; that she deserved better. I watched and listened to my parents and tried to think of questions but had no idea who to ask. I was on the outside, alone and powerless to change anything. I kept quiet and listened. She yelled, demanded, and argued, and my dad brought home boxes.

The only outcome was leaving everything we loved on Dixie Drive. Mom and I would each carry one side of a basket of clean laundry and hang on the clothesline in the sun, just the two of us. We talked about things, her school, my school, the news about people on our street, and the Holy Rollers, who'd become our friends. I loved getting in the big bathtub filled with warm water and bubbles, and getting out all cold and wet, quickly drying, putting on a clean nightgown, stiff from baking in the sun, stuffing damp arms into stubborn sleeves, and kneeling, softening the fabric by moving to pray before slipping between crisp, clean sheets to sleep. I loved my special room where I practiced ballet, read my books, wrote stories, and did my home-work. I felt like part of this house, with roots, grown through, under, and into this just right home.

When the moving truck was being loaded, I said goodbye to the "riffraff" on my street: my best friends and their families in the apart-ment. We cried, moms, kids hugging and promising to visit.

And the girl behind the fence.

She was looking out, watching us load. I hadn't seen her in a while, with school and trips away taking so much of my time. I walked to the edge of her fence. We held eyes, and as we walked closer to each other, I was shocked to see how her body had changed. She had a huge stomach. When we locked fingers, her right hand moved to her belly, and she broke into tears. She was barely twelve. With her head down and both hands grasping mine through the fence, she sobbed goodbye. We put our heads together. Her father slammed out through the screen door and yelled at her to get back into the house and get away from me. She looked hard into my eyes and smiled. She blew a kiss as she turned to run away, dodging his hand. I had a reaction to yell back at him to leave her alone, but I didn't . . . I was seven and in way over my head.

She was only safe and sound inside my prayers.

We moved into the new house on James Place in Pomona. It was on a paved street just like Mr. Stewart told me it would be. There were thick weeds and no fence in the backyard. Dad, in an angry voice, said he had no plans to build one. Poor Picket had to be tied up, and he hated it. I hated it.

Mr. Stewart arrived loud and grinning with a red bottle of something to celebrate and a pink flower for me. Not so sure about this. Picket would not stop barking at him.

I knew something wasn't right, and I just didn't know what.

Dad called my grandfather Earl, and they decided my dog would have to live at The Ranch. A new town, my dog leaving, a new school, no friends, I was mad. I was sad. So my mother called the doctor. He recommended I get some rest and told my parents to take it easy on me. I demanded Picket sleep in my room until he left. We snuggled like puppies, saying goodbye and his eyes making promises to see each other soon, my best friend in the world. Dad took Picket to The Ranch without me, saying it would be easier on me. I cried for a couple of days. My mother had a pretty keen eye and took me to the pet store. There, we saw a total ink-black kitten with bright blue eyes. I held her close, and it was done. Gypsy entered my life, a new kind of snuggle. I told her all about her brother Picket while she purred on my pillow.

That summer, my dad heard about a new thing — buy now and pay later. He went for it and brought home a TV with a grin. I was thrilled. We rearranged the living room. Dad climbed a ladder and set up the antenna on the roof, then raced down to make adjustments. I stood ready with tools in hand, eager for the black and white picture to appear. My mother came home. She was not happy at all. Dad spent money we didn't have.

I started new piano lessons, but Mom didn't like listening to me practice. In a huff, she'd scoot me over and expertly play the piece I was trying to learn. She'd say, "That's how to play it," leaving me silent and stunned every time it happened. She was tired and out of patience with both of us. It was the beginning of feeling bored. I was "below par," unimportant to an angry mom, and I was careful to not make a show of siding with my dad. My 8th birthday passed silently — my mom forgetting. My grandmothers and aunts sent cards, and my mom stormed, furious with herself, and blamed Dad.

I walked to the new school every day, even in the rare Southern California rain. The school was built with temporary buildings on a vast empty lot. All the kids were new, the school and the teachers were new. Surrounded by dirt, we loved every dusty, muddy minute. We had a wonderful teacher, and I found peace in the third grade. We raced to raise our hands and vied for attention. I felt safe and at home with my classmates but recess was the top of our day. The vacant lot was ours to turn from a playground into forts and wars, all based on the communist threat, cowboys, and Indians. I was steadfastly on the side of Indians. After all, I was one.

When I got home after school, I could watch television until my parents came home from work. When they did, they started to argue. I left to go to my room to play records and read to Gypsy.

As the year went by, tensions rose at home over money. So, my dad got another job to ease the tension at night. He was the second shift engineering supervisor at a manufacturing plant that got a large government contract. He'd get home at 1am, then he'd sleep enough to get up and go to work as a teacher, then drive to the plant after school. He was exhausted and touchy. I tiptoed around, being careful not to inflame the already raging fire.

For Christmas, I got a new bicycle, a blue two-wheeler. It remained just a bike with no name. I took out my anger in the streets that begged for racing. I left, I rode, I quit crying. I got mad. I also hit a rock and went flying. A neighbor saw my accident and took me to her home for repairs to my face. My parents weren't home, and I knew I'd broken the rules. When my mother got home after work, she took me to the hospital for fifteen stitches on my jaw. The next morning, I got to stay home and listen to them yell and blame each other for not watching me. I lost all privilege for the rest of my life.

The summer before I turned nine, vacation started with an argument. Our family focused on the threat of Mr. Stewart, my mother's job as his secretary, and my father's jealousy and shaky relationship with money. She didn't play the piano anymore, he moped and yelled, and I dodged whatever slings and arrows flew through our new fancy house in the kind of neighborhood that Mom deserved.

Things slowed to a simmer when Dad agreed to get a summer job after school ended to pay off the "god-damned television."

I could hear their loud conversations, and I was beginning to understand. I agreed about Mr. Stewart. He spent too much time at our house. I always scooted into my room when he arrived and when my mom called for me to come out and say hello, I had a good reason to stay put.

Years later, she told me she fell in love with her boss and had a "little affair." Coming to terms with her imagined glamorous life with Mr. Stewart balanced with disappointment in the man she married threw her off her game. It confused and angered my dad and left me to survive alone.

Mom had an expanded view of herself, and when she was flattered by men, like Mr. Stewart, she ignored us. She became obsessed with her weight, exercise, and her figure. Dieting was a constant subject, and she decided it would be "fun" to track my weight and measurements, too. She kept the records in a little book she held in her underwear drawer.

Dad's summer day job was being a mechanical engineer at the new Disneyland Park in Anaheim. I was so happy when we saw the park being built each week on "The Wonderful World of Disney" on TV.

I tried my best at eight years old to do what I could to keep us safe. Not complain, do well in school, help with chores and dinner, and always do the dishes so they could talk. Oddly, it was the TV that brought some lightness to these two, and they started to laugh.

In July, one month before my ninth birthday and almost a year after the big move, the builders and engineers' families were invited to a free day before the park opened. Dad and I went. The television was paid off, and we had the time of our lives. He rode every ride where he fit and explored every corner of every land. We ate hamburgers and ice cream. Nothing could have been better to fill in the cracks in our family.

When we got home, Mom announced that her school papers were done, ready to turn in, and it was time we took a vacation.

Just us three, no more Mr. Stewart.

ACT II

If I Should Die Before I Wake

Thirteen

Camping

I was in the back seat of my parent's car, waiting in a slow line of traffic with hundreds of tourists. I watched steam pouring out of multiple hot spots in the field ahead as heat shimmered on the road to the entrance of Yellowstone National Park. I turned my head to the right and saw a big brown bear amble up to the window — my window. His nose was close, and he breathed snotty goop on the glass. He opened his mouth and twisted his head from side to side. Slobber sneaked out of his open mouth, and I shivered.

Dad said, "That's a brown bear. It's called a grizzly, and it's a deadly beast."

"Ursus arctos horribilis," Mom read a pamphlet warning us not to feed the bears. "The common brown grizzly bear populating Yellowstone park, along with the black bear: Ursus americanus. Yellowstone is one of the few areas south of Canada where black bears coexist with the grizzly bears."

Throwing his head to the right, Dad, watching the road ahead with one eye, added, "You can't predict their behavior. They look cute, but they're cold-blooded killers."

I counted 25 "Don't Feed the Bears" signs on our way to the park that day. It made a lot of sense. A bear could bite down on your hand, then pull you through the window and carry you away like a dead rabbit.

They studied regional history and geography, both current and extinct native plants, peoples, and animals. They lectured important facts during the drive to make the trip more interesting . . . for each other. Mom kept up the flow of information as we inched our way to the campground entrance on a highway crowded with tourists, forest rangers, and bears — lots of bears.

Our car pulled a teardrop trailer. It was filled with neatly packed camping supplies and a mattress that slept two adults. Mom had explained the plan with precision while she directed the packing at home. The plan? I had to sleep in the back seat of the car.

"It's very safe, darling . . . nothing to worry about. We'll be quite close. And besides, you will learn so much, you can write a wonderful little story on your summer vacation. If you get scared, you can honk the horn. It will be so fun."

This was my first annoying camping trip with my parents. They acted like this was the most meaningful exploration ever done in the Western United States. I remember being worried at the end of Mom's talk. But, I had to trust her. I had no choice.

We turned at the entrance from the road leading to the Yellowstone campground, showed our pass to the rangers, and began the winding drive through the campsites. These two parents loved to pretend we were days away from civilization, re-enacting what it must have been like at the "first" western campsite. I was eight and could see lots of people camping and thought the idea was kind of silly, but I went along.

After dinner, I helped mom wash the metal camping dishes in water heated over the campfire while dad whittled small branches into spikes for roasting marshmallows. Mom began the lecture for the night as we all gazed at the crystal clear sky.

"Now remember, look for shooting stars tonight. They're really giant boulders called meteors, flying at super high speed. When they hit the earth's atmosphere, they start to glow from the heat of friction between the mass of the object and the speed of its entry into the moist atmosphere."

Looking up, I imagined a sky filled with shooting stars.

⌇

"Sometimes they can burn so hot they explode, and sometimes when the asteroid is very dense, it will hit the earth."

I was so excited to eat toasted marshmallows and watch for shooting stars far away from civilization, listening to Mom's educational lesson on meteors — maybe it would be just like Lewis and Clark.

"Loren, please grab the extra pillow for our girl."

Mom was setting up my bed in the back seat of the car. It looked cozy. Mom said, "Now, here's a cup."

"Remember, if you have to go to the bathroom, don't leave the car and use the cup."

I knew the routine — going in a cup was a high camping skill. Mom told stories about the trips they took before I was eight. The handy cup was used in a surprise snowstorm in Canada, in the bushes being cautious of poison ivy, in a tent next to a creek listening to howling wolves.

I worried about spilling it in the car but kept quiet.

Mom continued the list, "No matter what — do not leave the car for any reason. Never, ever roll down the windows or open the door. If you feel afraid, honk the horn, and we'll come to get you."

Dad added with gruff confidence, his hands in his pockets to ward off the chill, "No bear is going to get my girl."

Swell. I should feel safe. My parents were expert campers. Right?

They acted experienced and certainly counted on me to play my part — a good, polite, happy, fearless, and cooperative child.

I wasn't so sure.

The campfire had been extinguished with Smokey the Bear efficiency, and all the bear slobber was cleaned off the windows. I watched them walk to the trailer hand in hand. They turned and waved goodnight — it felt creepy, like they were saying goodbye.

I looked at the huge black sky with stars and more stars. Some were larger, and some were smaller . . . I lost myself in a night-time kind of daydream trying to figure out the best way to count them — how long will it take to get to a billion . . . then fell asleep.

BAM skitter, roll, clatter, *BAM*.

I woke with a start, "What was that?"

With sharp eyes and fast breath, I looked out the window, trying to figure out what the noise was. I couldn't see anything. It was cold in the car parked on the opposite side of the site, far enough from the camper. I was in a blacked-out forest filled with things I couldn't imagine. Remembering Mom's instructions, I snuggled in and waited for the next sound, eyes open — wide, wide awake.

There was a sharp knock on the window. It was light. I almost cried with relief. I sat up and saw my smiling mother motioning me to unlock the door. I got out of the car, and my mom gave me a big hug for being brave.

"How is my almost 9-year-old girl? Did you sleep all right? You looked just like a snug bug in a rug."

Over breakfast, I excitedly told them all about the sky and stars, counting to a million, and the noises I heard, dramatizing the "bam skitter roll clatter and bam." Dad explained that chipmunks dropped their pine cones on the car. Sure enough, the mangled pine cones were scattered on the ground.

"Those pesky chipmunks, they love to scare eight-year-old girls."

They laughed at my adventure while Dad cooked bacon in a pan over a glowing campfire, and my mom poured more coffee in her cup. The meal was amazing. Mom's pancakes, eggs, and thick bacon were camp food heaven. She set a steaming cup of hot milk, sugar, and cocoa in front of me and said, "Today, my darling, we will tour the geysers Yellowstone is known for. There are over 10,000 hot springs and geysers in this park, and we'll try to see them all."

I waited for the protest to Mom's plan, and right on time, it came from Dad, "Oh no, we won't. If we do, we may never get home."

I sipped my hot cup of cocoa in the warm morning light and listened.

Back from the exploration, we parked in the campsite after a long monologue of geysers, facts, more geysers, and more facts. I helped gather all the trash littering the car and got ready for lunch. Mom opened the aluminum insulated cooler with bear locks on each side.

"Mr. Jones said this cooler is guaranteed to withstand bears." Dad quoted his friend at the camping store with puffed-up confidence as Mom assembled ham sandwiches, carrot sticks, and chips. We sat down at the picnic table, locked the food container, and started to eat. Mom listed the itinerary for the afternoon, "We should see Mammoth Hot Springs. It's a rather long trip, but we'll drive back at twilight. It will be so pretty," she added romantically.

Dad scoffed, "Oh, you'll think it's really pretty when it gets so dark we get lost."

I heard a rustle of leaves and looked around my laughing parents, who were still teasing each other. Out from behind a small, dense group of young pine trees came two cute little ears followed by the face of a baby bear sniffing the air. I couldn't tell if it was dangerous or if it was a black or brown bear because of the shade. I said with a small voice, "Dad, there's a baby bear in the trees behind you."

"What?" he said with a mouthful of a ham sandwich and worry on his face.

I said it again, "There's a baby bear in the trees behind you."

Dad said in a low, urgent, directive voice, "Where there's a baby, there's always a mother. Get up slowly, keep your eyes down, and slowly back up to the car. NOW!"

Our little party moved out from behind the table, walked backward slowly, sandwich plates in hand, step by step. Then, midway to the car, silent, stealthy, and with no warning, the mother bear appeared. She turned her large black, furry body and looked at us. She snorted, rolled her head, and stood straight up.

I was frozen in place, my mind blank . . . She was right in front of us — paws in the air, nose sniffing with interest.

"Get in the car — get in the car," my dad whisper-yelled.

We turned and stumbled frantically into the car. As my mother turned to lock her door, she placed her paper plate, with a half-eaten sandwich, on the driver's seat. Dad skidded into the car and sat as the bear announced in a chilling roar that she was the boss. I leaned over the front seats to watch in amazement as the mother and baby bear tore through the campsite. Mom, the explorer, was weeping, and Dad sat in stunned silence as the mother bear popped the bear-proof locks off the food chest as if they were pretzels. Then she hooked her claws under the edge of the chest and bent the top back like a sardine can as the baby happily romped over to eat.

As we watched, the mother bear twisted the top off a jar of mayonnaise and stuck her tongue into the jar. She cleaned it out with one sloppy swipe and then tossed it over her black furry shoulder. Coming out of his stunned silence, my dad started the car and said, "We have to get a ranger right now."

Driving fast, we skidded into the ranger station. Dad turned off the car and said urgently, "Wait for me here." As he got out of the car, the paper plate with the squished ham sandwich fell off his butt. Mom covered her mouth and gasped, "My dear, you are thoroughly covered in ham sandwich."

Dad turned, screwed up a frown on his face, and yelled, "What?"

Laughing uncontrollably, we watched as Dad picked the food off the back of his tan shorts. With a look of great dramatic courage, he marched toward the ranger station with mustard and a missed piece of lettuce still on his butt.

The Ranger led us back to the destroyed campsite. It was trampled. The food from the cooler was flung everywhere, and the picnic table was overturned — it looked hopeless. The bears were still walking around snuffling around the site when the Ranger got out of his Jeep, took a gun out of his holster, and shot it over the trees. Everybody jumped.

He yelled, "Mary, get the hell out of here."

As a group, we looked at him in jaw-dropping amazement. It was the last thing we expected to hear. Mary? This big-mouthed, slathering beast was named Mary?

The Ranger turned to us while the bears ambled away from the campsite and said, "She can be a bit of trouble now and then. She seems to have gotten braver since she had her cub."

We looked at him with wide-eyed disbelief as he dryly announced, "You folks need a new campsite."

Fourteen

The Jazz Act

A talent show was announced in the fall of fourth grade, and I signed up on my own, no permission, just me. I was nine, the piano was my instrument, and I felt confident and wanted more than anything to participate.

I was convinced I could do what they did, my parents the professional jazz performers.

We practiced for their performances, my mom at the piano, and me taking the harmony in my kid voice singing at the top of our lungs. Mom wrote in my baby book that my ability to carry a tune was remarkable. Dad played the drums in the band and practiced in the garage with the door open. He coordinated the rhythm to each piece we were practicing. Inspired by the records of Gene Krupa, the legendary jazz drummer, he gave it his all. Neighbors walked by our house and stopped to listen. My neighborhood classmates were impressed with our family activity and hung around dancing and punching each other.

I knew I could do it.

When the school talent show was announced and a signup sheet was passed around, I didn't hesitate to put my name down and list the piano as my act. I saw what other kids were doing: baton twirling, tap dancing, and hilarious ventriloquism from the funniest boy in class. I was so excited to see my name on the list with the other kids.

My confidence grew.

I went to my piano lessons and told my teacher what I planned. She was tickled. She gave me suggestions for my piece in the program, and we wrote the notes on a music manuscript. She gave me lots of tips and piano exercises to practice, so my original piece was laid out. I was diligent and practiced every day after school.

When my parents came home one day after teaching and heard me practicing my piano lessons, they commented sarcastically, "Boy, I hope these lessons are worth it!" They laughed with each other as if it was funny, and I kept practicing. I worried it would be a massacre of bad jokes and the reminder that I had small "t" talent and shouldn't set myself up to fail. I didn't tell them I'd signed up to play in public.

The program was printed and distributed to students and teachers. When I took it home, my parents gasped! Mom struggled to speak without losing herself, "But you don't *really* play the piano — my God, you can't play in public."

I was a little intimidated but equally convinced this was my moment to shine. In movies, I'd seen the one in the back, the one no one notices, the one who gets her chance. With a deep breath, the actress opens her mouth or sits at the piano and dazzles the audience.

I knew I wasn't in a movie, but as I stood in hearing range of my mom's call to the school, I prayed I could have a chance to dazzle my parents. She called and pleaded the case that I should be taken out of the program, but it was too late.

I felt a little worried, but maybe, just maybe they would be thrilled.

With exasperation, my mom rolled my hair into pin curls, polished my black patent leather Mary Jane shoes, ironed and starched my favorite dress. All the while, she verbalized dread at her potential humiliation balanced with "we believe in you" platitudes. I was vaguely concerned about how good I had to be to avoid their humiliation. At the least, I needed to look great.

At the assembly, I waited my turn backstage. We were all together in a loose group waiting for the program to start. The boys acted silly. "Boys, boys," the annoyed music teacher said in a loud whisper that made the boys laugh. I got compliments on my dress and curly hair.

The girls wanted to touch it because my mom used hair spray. We rustled in a small group, glancing at the stage and up at our teacher.

One by one, we performers were called to move out to the stage in front of the assembled parents. Each kid performed and came backstage to applause even if a baton was dropped or a song had to be started over. The ventriloquism had the audience of parents, families, and friends howling with laughter.

My name was called, and I walked out to polite applause in my starched dress and freshly done hair. The stage light felt warm, the place felt powerful, and the stage was right for me. I sat down at the piano, took a deep, meaningful breath, and started to play the discordant, original jazz tune I had authored. I played with gusto, remembering every note. When I finished with a dramatic chord, I sat there with my head down, letting the ending moment sink in. There was silence. I mistook it for awe. I took a breath, stood up, and curtsied to scattered applause. But, like magic, the applause grew and grew, and a few people were standing up and whistling.

I looked for my parents in the audience. My heart swelled, and I knew I'd done it. I found them. In the midst of a clapping, smiling, and enthusiastic audience, their faces were locked in shock and horror. My dad's eyes were huge, and his mouth hung open. My mother's hands covered her face as she moved her head from side to side.

I was confused — this wasn't at all what I thought would happen, not even close.

I went offstage with my head held high, tears sneaking out of my eyes and dripping down my cheeks. The teachers backstage were laughing and hugging me for being so funny, cute, and brave. The kids were laughing and telling me how good it was. Maybe I was good. Confused and worried, I met my parents backstage. My mother, with a forced public smile on her face, pinched my arm and said in a loud hush, "How could you? You embarrassed us." Shockwaves covered me, sound went away, and I could hardly think or breathe.

I was banished from our piano, lessons canceled until I got some "sense of proportion," a word I had to look up. My parents continued to be professional jazz musicians and highly praised history teachers. Their reputations weren't tarnished after all. I listened for hints of humiliation in the conversations they had after work and on the phone. I wasn't embarrassed at school, everyone at school simply forgot, and I lost interest in the piano.

After the glorious disaster, my parents had their odd child, me, tested with a psychologist. By this time in my life, I was at the mercy of their dramatic decisions.

It wouldn't end here; it was just the beginning. It was just another thing in the vast litany of choices they made about their not-so-right daughter. Until I entered junior high, she had my IQ tested every year. I wasn't only normal, I was a very smart and well-adjusted kid, the daughter of a fixer, a daughter who didn't need fixing.

I started to think about the reality. I might have made mistakes and embarrassed myself, but it would be me. I did need my parents, I was still a member of the trio, and I had to learn how to live in it. I was new at this kind of thinking and not very good at self-preservation, but at this point, a light went on. Win, lose, or land in the middle, I could survive — maybe.

It was a good thing because junior high and high school were around the corner, and I would need the strength.

As the weeks and months went by, I lost the talent vision, and I began to play the clarinet. In a way, I was becoming brave. I loved their parental groans as I practiced and silently dared them to cancel my lessons. Making sure I had perspective, my dad bought two second-hand Pete Fountain records and pointed out a well-played clarinet. I wasn't great, not too bad, just average, but good enough. I auditioned for the sixth grade band, and by the time I entered junior high, I was okay. I really cared about being in the band. We had uniforms, learned how to march on a field and in Christmas parades. It was fun — a safe place for me to live on my mother's scale of accomplishment. She relaxed. I learned to cope with the knowledge that being mediocre was the middle line. It wasn't a failure.

Our musical life did go on. I went with my parents to rehearsals, tryouts for band members and singers, and production planning. Concerts were the best. I could invite friends to sit in the audience, and sometimes the backstage girls in hair and makeup would playfully add pink lipstick and cheek color to my face. It was fun, and I felt part of it.

One night, a single spotlight framed the slim curvy woman, beautiful in a shimmering blue gown. She was tall and stood before red velvet curtains as she caressed a microphone stand with red-tipped fingernails. Taking a long, deep breath, she absorbed the moment, and just before the music from the orchestra pit swept to the stage, she started to sing. Her voice filled the theater with warmth and complexity as it rolled, then soared and dipped with the musicians into *My Funny Valentine*.

She finished, paused, her head bowed down, the lights came up, and the audience was on their feet. Applause and shouts of "Bravo!" "Brava!" filled the theater. She put her right hand over her heart and bowed again as cries of "encore" rose to the ornate ceiling. A young tux-wearing man walked up the side stairs and presented her with a bouquet of roses. He gently escorted her off, stage left.

She was a star, not a big one but big enough to sing at the Hollywood Bowl and just about fill the Orpheum Theater in LA. I remember leaning over a balcony railing to watch the fans in the audience. These people were nuts about her, or maybe their idea of who she was.

I have a clearer vision of the fan dynamic now, looking back at the creature that was my mother. They seemed to need to be close to a sparkling thing. My mother explained that fans' lives were drab and commonplace, and she gave them something to perk them up.

I knew my place. I reflected her marvelous self, on the outside edge in the shadows, in the back of the balcony, waiting.

Then I wished for just a bit of the blissful elevation, when she focused on me, for the tiniest minute, when I could relax and forget to keep my eyes open.

⌘

Armed with piles of books, homework assignments, and writing paper, I was a witness to rehearsals and parties where adults smoked, drank cocktails, swore at each other, then eventually broke into a jazz piece. Mom and her best friend would harmonize and scat. There was flirting and the one woman all men paid attention to was my mother.

One hot Los Angeles day, we drove with windows open, in our non-air conditioned car, to a show production meeting in Los Angeles. The home was located in the hills above the city. It was so much nicer than ours on James Place. If only Mr. Stewart could see this one . . .

This classy home was occupied by the man who played trumpet in the orchestra. I had homework, and it was my dad's job to find a place for me to study and stay put. I was free to sneak closer to the action because no one cared about "the kid" once I was placed. There were drinks leaving water stains in haphazard circles on the dining room table or on the kitchen counter. The music and side conversations were loud in the background. I slinked into the kitchen to pick gin-soaked olives off toothpicks left in abandoned cocktail glasses.

I heard my mom's laughter and moved soundlessly down the hall, following her voice. I stood bravely behind a door and watched her. She posed with her bare legs crossed, on a round ottoman, surrounded by drunk and smoking men who laughed and vied for attention from this seductive creature. Her red hair was piled on top of her head. Her sleeveless blouse was tied at her slim waist and topped yellow shorts. She leaned back on one arm and gestured, accenting her conversation with her other hand. I felt uncomfortable. Was this thing part of performing?

I moved to look for my father and saw him laughing with other people on the other side of the room. I had an idea about what was going on, but the only place I could have seen this kind of action was in the movies.

I felt nervous — as if something was going to happen, like Mr. Stewart. Could I stop the thing if I saw it this time? Could I tap dance and change the direction of our trio if I saw it? Could I distract them with my clarinet and marching skills?

For a time, I watched my parent's every move, waiting.

Fifteen

Blessed is the Fruit

You are either baptized, or you aren't. Reverend Francis Ellis blessed the water, dripped it on my then five-year-old head, and said the words:

> *"Go ye therefore, and make disciples of all nations,*
> *baptizing them in the name of the Father, and of the*
> *Son, and of the Holy Ghost."*

The words changed my status and magically gave me permission to "go ye therefore." This special occasion took place at the San Dimas Community Church. The reverend had hired my mother as the soloist to improve attendance in this growing Protestant-multi-denominational church. In attendance at my baptism were my grandparents, Earl and Edna, who drove down the state from The Ranch in Central California. Mom's Catholic brother Everett Redmond and his wife Joanne came with my noisy baby infant cousin Johnny and made the sign of the cross after every prayer. I immediately adopted the sign of the cross. My father stopped me and said, "We aren't Catholic. You can only do the sign of the cross if you're baptized in their church."

Mom ordered flowers and did what she could afford to make it memorable, and she sang the solo. The local small-town newspaper gushed about the production and the soloist. I remember the dress and the shoes and the adorable pillow I knelt upon. Also, I got a certificate and a Revised Standard Version of the Holy Bible with Helps. Mom had the certificate framed for my bedroom wall, and the Bible is still in my bookcase.

In 5th grade, I could say "yes" to the question, "Are you baptized?" I was in the "in" group. In school, I tried to dominate other kids with that question. We who had been baptized and sang "Onward Christian Soldiers" at recess ruled. The scheme was harmless for the most part because everyone said "yes" until I met Evelyn. She took one look at me and my pitiful question and said, "No, I'm a Russian, and I'm a Jew."

Russian? I had so many questions I nearly levitated on the spot.

"Weren't Soviets Russian?"

"No! Don't be silly; they're different."

How is that possible? Didn't we duck and cover because of the Soviet threat of nuclear war? Didn't we pledge to never talk if a Communist told us to confess? Who are the Russians?

I had to know more. Evelyn's serious, freckled face broke into a dimpled smile when I asked her to sit with me at lunch. I was curious about this exotic creature. We became instant friends, faith, or no faith, and she was steadfast against Soviet communism. Whew.

I told her about the "pledge" we created and signed in second grade. We spoke about our childish understanding of Jewishness and Christianity, democracy, and communism. The distinctions between religion and politics didn't seem so different since we used fifth grade logic. When she said Jesus was a Jew, I almost choked. I got over it quickly, but I could not wait to check that fact with my family.

I went to her house after school to do homework. Her grandmother always had some wonderful sweet fried dough thing to eat. We hugged and laughed every day, held hands, competed hard in spelling and math, and stayed best of friends until her family moved to New York. I lost a sister, a friend, a comrade.

The summer I was eleven, I went to work with and attended mass by my grandmother Lalan Redmond's side. She was a devout Catholic, and we attended mass every day. She grew up protestant in Tennessee, but things changed when she came to California with four sisters, looking for a new way of life. Her conversion to Catholicism followed her son's passionate plea, my uncle Everett, after WWII, before I was born. Her daughter, my mother, Ina Mae, said, "There is nothing more annoying than a convert."

Lalan's dazzling cooking skills and dedicated devotion to her church got her the job cooking for St. Elizabeth Catholic Church and school in Van Nuys, a town just outside the city of Los Angeles. She cooked three meals a day for the priests who said mass and the nuns who taught school.

Mass was regimented, musical, beautiful, and we kneeled to pray. My grandmother allowed me to do the sign of the cross even though I wasn't yet baptized in the Catholic Church. I loved the ancient ritual. I had a rosary and learned how to recite every prayer linked to each section of the beads. It felt historical and legitimate, like a museum in Rome. I felt at home.

At daily confession, I watched my grandmother slowly walk, with her head down in prayer, into the confessional. What sins could she possibly have committed? I was so curious. Plus, I wanted to confess all my sins: The act of contrition, confession, and penance. As a kid, I lied and had done sneaky things. I got so excited to tell. I wanted rules and law to fall down on what felt wrong. However, the confessional path was to 1) complete catechism, then 2) attend my first communion. It took time, and I didn't think I had enough.

Summers with Lalan were as disciplined as she was. I was her assistant in the meal preparation and her student learning what I needed to know to convert. I grew strong as my lessons progressed. There were answers and rules here, procedure, and ritual. We'd rise before dawn and drive to the church, unlock the service door, turn on the lights, and light the giant black iron stove. I had a list of duties for preparing breakfast. Our aprons stained, coffee perking, fresh juice chilling, and daily bread set aside to rise when we both finished. We swept into the chapel for mass and confession and then hurried back to the kitchen. I learned to serve, and as my skills improved, I was warmly enveloped by the nuns. They called me "Our Girl of the Kitchen."

Lalan never tired of watching and gently correcting my technique, prayers, and parroting the finer points of Catholic dogma. I became stronger, more certain. My ability to follow directions and instructions improved. I thrived.

The summer I turned thirteen, the cooking test and final acceptance into catechism came at the same time. She'd taught me poaching, braising, sauces, chopping/dicing, and the last lesson was pastry. It was to be judged. The priests were set up as judges, and I had a week, seven days to complete the cake and pass the test.

The cake was tricky. Part of the milk, flour, and egg yolks was simmered into custard and cooled. The cream was heated and poured over chopped chocolate. The remaining dry ingredients and egg yolks were added in a delicate operation. Three egg whites were whisked by hand into peaks in a copper bowl. The whites were gently folded into the cooled chocolate batter. The layers had to be even, frosted and chilled twice.

It was too much for me. I gave up the first day. A priest walked into the room, took one look at me and my failed effort, and left me standing there covered in chocolate frustration without speaking.

Lalan calmly showed me how to clean it up and start again. By the second day, I refused, gave up, and refused again, yet I wasn't allowed to quit. I couldn't quit. I wouldn't quit.

I made a cake every day. One or two priests would come in, walk around the cake, and speak in Latin, so I didn't know what they were saying. I stood next to my tiny grandmother in my stained apron as the priests wagged their heads no. On Saturday afternoon, the final cake came out of the oven looking good. Cooled, I trimmed the tops flat and made the frosting. I frosted the crumb layer, chilled, and then smoothed the sides of the cake with thick chocolate buttercream, swooping the top. It felt good. I was amazed. I knew I'd done it. Father Peter walked in and stopped. He looked at my grandmother, and she offered him a napkin, plate, and fork. She cut the cake, handed it slowly to him. He took a bite and savored it dramatically. He turned a bit to the right and winked at me. He declared it perfect and called "Yes" out loud, and all the other priests piled in to congratulate me and finally eat cake.

My dear grandmother Redmond believed that failure, though time-consuming, was valuable. "What you eventually learn, you can never unlearn."

When I got home, leaving St. Elizabeth and my grandmother Lalan behind, I worried about my conversion plan and wished I lived closer to my grandmother. I wanted to go to St. Elizabeth School with my favorite nuns. When school started that year, I asked a Catholic friend about catechism, and she said I could come to her church and sign up. Satisfied, I tried to work out the plan without consulting my mother.

One afternoon, just before dinner, as I was setting the table, the phone rang. I answered, and it was my grandmother Lalan. She asked to talk with my mom, who took the call in her bedroom.

I heard my mother yelling . . .

"Never, ever can you use my daughter . . . She will never become Catholic. Never . . . "

"Stay away from her. She is not yours . . . This is the last summer she stays with you."

My plans came to a screeching halt.

ᴖᴖ

The summer I turned 13 was going to be spent in Lindsay at The Ranch with my Brethren grandparents, Edna and Earl Shryer. My dog Picket was waiting for me, and I was old enough to ride the train by myself. Mom and Dad took me to Union Station in Los Angeles, urging me to write about my experience. I smiled, wondering if Mom forgot I was too old to write my summer story. I listened to all the instructions and followed every rule. They said, "Bye, bye sweetheart!" They waved, threw kisses, held hands, and literally skipped away.

That summer, I started to pay attention to what was going on around me. I was a little unnerved. My grandmother, Edna, and other Brethren women in the church plotted which boy should be my husband.

"Well, Janet, dear, you are becoming a lovely young woman." Edna casually mused about my maturing body, factually like it was a changing season.

I didn't think much about being a woman, but I'd been told, instructed, and reminded that I should expect a "big" change soon.

"Your 'monthly' will start in the next couple of years, and it's a very important time for a woman. Blessed is the fruit of your womb," my grandmother said in a whisper.

I felt like a 4-H breeding heifer being groomed to auction.

The family church of my father, the Brethren Church of Strathmore, was founded by my great-grandfather Jacob Mishler. The community had strict guidelines for behavior and gender roles. With a truth firmly fixed in the New Testament, the place girls held in this order of life were clear. We were a commodity, and church women moved us around like pieces on a conversational chessboard.

"Oh, I think Patty would be perfect for the Miller boy. He's getting tall and strong."

Give us all a break. The poor boy had terminal acne and the worst breath in the universe.

"I'm sure Susie is perfect for the Gottschaller boy. They would have such beautiful babies."

Susie didn't seem happy about any boys, for that matter, and the Gottschaller boy looked like a frightened woodland faun.

They picked a boy for me — a huge, hairy guy in thigh-high mud boots who invited me over to his family farm to milk cows. My grandmother enthusiastically dropped me off. Seriously? His parents were sweet, eager, and hopeful. I was polite but clear about being a Presbyterian from LA, trying to become Catholic, not one of the Brethren from Strathmore. They just smiled and nodded as if they didn't speak English.

I did well milking the sweet cows. They seemed calm around me, and the huge guy was impressed enough to comment I'd be a good farm wife. I was silent. While sweetly smiling, I seriously thought about running out to the highway and hitchhiking home. My head rested on the belly of a warm cow as I prayed for my grandmother

Edna to mind-read and come rescue me. I felt a little panic. I could end up married to this guy, and I had no power to stop it . . . yet.

Edna arrived just in time to seal the deal when I quickly moved to the car and asked to leave. She was a little thrown by my urgency, yet she agreed to take me home. I could never be what my grandparents wanted for me and I think she knew. I waved at the surprised family as we lifted dust, driving me out of hell.

Every day of the week had Brethren activity. We went to potlucks with Jell-O salads, creamed celery casserole, green beans, potato salad, fried chicken, and prayer circles. Youth group summer outings were normal and kind of fun, but foot washing on Wednesday nights in the basement of the Brethren Church was just plain creepy.

My grandmother Edna quoted scripture:

"If I then, your Lord and Teacher, have washed your feet, you also ought to wash one another's feet." – John 13:14

She spoke of foot washing with such grandeur and the passion for meaningful service. Who could refuse? She believed that the humble, loving action of foot washing was a symbolic removal of status, equal in the eyes of a loving God. I got the point and was inspired by her fond interpretation of equality though I felt stuck in a thing I had to do.

Some of us young women, who belonged to the Youth Group of the Brethren Church, dreaded foot washing, while others had a firm grip on the high ground of biblical service. We who felt the dread of being in the basement, circled by strangers, had to trust. These were members of the church, and we were united. They were good, Godly, reverent, solid people of the earth. We, silent doubters, took strength from the most dedicated girls in our group and stood in a prayer circle, earnestly holding hands, silently asking for the wishes of those who would be sacrificed: swift action and memory loss. One of the girls prayed, "God give us grace. We pray the humble love of Jesus enters our hearts as we prepare for this loving communion."

I couldn't put the words of that prayer nor my grandmother's firm belief in service on the same list as kneeling in front of and touching farmer feet.

There were no boys — just girls.

It was strange.

We were dressed to look sweet.

We were told to be silent and giving.

We walked heads down into the basement, hearts beating, and each stood in front of one of the farmers or wives, their footwear removed, bare feet beside a metal bowl, and pitchers filled with water. We knelt in front of a bowl and prayed, "God give us grace," and a gross pair of feet went in the bowl. We poured water over the feet then dried them with an ironed white cloth. The basement was heavy with praying, the mixed smell of feet, cologne, and the splashes of washing. We did what was expected.

I always fought tears. I felt like I was in the wrong place. It was sick.

If one of us got one or another of the men, some petting and stroking would be disguised as a blessing. A slip of the hand from a praying man, rough farmer fingers, calloused from work could just graze your back or lightly brush the side of your chest as he helped you rise to the next pair of feet. The women were so sweet and thankful. They hugged us after the weekly ceremony, and we didn't tell them if it was their husband who "stroked."

When we gathered after the event and before we went into the main church service, I stood still, apart from the group. I watched as the girls comforted each other and told the grossest stories they could come up with. I knew the feeling of the half-closed eyes of a man looking at you as if foot-washing was something on the charred edge of wrong.

∾

The Strathmore Brethren Church's main building was a white wooden structure with a cross on the top of the peaked roof. The irrigation system for the property included a whitewashed concrete rectangular irrigation trough. Baptisms were held in this deep trough of cold water, which stood in for a river. When a thirteen-year-old girl stood in it, the water was chest high.

Every Sunday, I went with my grandparents to church and Sunday school. I was with other near teens my age. One Sunday, after we finished Sunday School and got ready to attend the full church service, I found out that my grandmother Edna had set me up for a "river dunk" that very summer. Some of the girls were giddy and excited about my new life as one of the Brethren. I was horrified and could not wait to confront my beloved grandmother. *Look, I'm from Southern California, and I'm not going to be a farmer's wife. I go to the Presbyterian Church where my friends go, nobody touches or bathes each other, and no one ever gets dunked in a thin white dress in public.* I didn't tell her my plan to become Catholic. I had a sense that there was an age when I could make decisions for myself, but it wasn't this summer, being baptized a second time and dating a boy from a dairy. It made no sense to me.

This baptism into The Brethren was orchestrated in righteousness and practiced in the United States since 1723. My grandparents Earl and Edna knew what I had to do to ensure I was on the right path. They thought baptism was urgent, an essential event for a young lady in the fold of history. Besides, Edna knew my mother would object.

I pleaded my case.

"I've been baptized already. You were there! I have a certificate on my wall at home to prove it. I don't need two. Where in the Bible does it say I need two?"

I teared up and knew I was sunk. Grandmother Edna was not moved by my plea. She'd attended my first drip, and just like that, she invalidated it, "You are ripe and ready to be a young lady. You belong in the fold."

My parents were on a camping trip in Canada, and it would all be done by the time they found out. Would she yell at Edna like she yelled at Lalan? Would she keep me away from The Ranch? Both grandmothers had plans for me, but I was desperate to carve my own path. My only option was to live through this summer and get home.

The dunking Sunday arrived, and I wore white. My grandmother had painstakingly made a dress for me out of a sheet. How could this be happening? She loved me and wanted this to be perfect for her young, almost woman. She added white lace around the hem and elastic wrists. She bought white shoes and socks and tied my hair with a white bow.

My mind slipped into sacrificial lamb kind of feelings.

But, I found strength in knowing this would all be over, I would be safe, and I could get on with life. It would be a good story for my non-touching, non-farming Presbyterian friends at home. And that's what I put in my mind when the preacher prayed and invited me with his outstretched hand to come closer and lead me to the irrigation trough. I stepped in while the blessed Brethren gathered around the trough, sang, and prayed. The preacher turned me away from him, my back to his chest, and pulled me close to his body while he preached. I could feel his body get hard, on my back, beneath the water. I was confused but didn't want to know about what was happening. It felt wrong. He put his hands on my head and lowered us deeply into the water. Up and down, repeat. I wanted to jump out screaming. He said words and felt my small breasts as if I was slipping. I wasn't. I choked and came up sputtering. I don't remember his words. I remember his hands.

The surrounding congregation's positive reaction was beautiful, and voices rose in a hymn as he pulled me close and hugged me. I had to get out fast before I threw up and spoiled everything. The church ladies surrounded me with loving laughter and covered my nearly transparent garment with a blanket. The ladies took me somewhere to get dry and dressed. I gagged. I knew I didn't do anything to make him do what he did. But what did I do wrong? It must have been a mistake. Maybe a slip of a hand? How could I tell anyone? Who would believe me?

When the ladies left, a few of the girls came into the room and asked me what I felt. It was a question that required an answer. I said, "It was a little weird."

One of the girls asked, "Did he touch you?"

We stood there looking at each other like a hand grenade had just dropped at our feet. We were quiet, then Molly meekly asked, "Did you feel Jesus in your soul?"

I was mad, and I hid it.

Hanna said, "The spirit should have entered your Christian heart." Right, it was the last thing I thought about. But I said, "Of course, Hanna, of course." Molly locked eyes with me and knew it wasn't true. She knew.

I told my grandmother the next day. In the kitchen.

She spun around, looked at me, eye to eye, and said, "What did you say?" Wiping her hands on a dishtowel, she scowled and spoke slowly, "Tell me the truth. Tell me again."

The eyes of Jesus in the picture on the wall seemed to look straight through me. I frantically thought maybe I was wrong; I must be wrong. I cried like I was guilty of lying. I took a breath, stood strong, and told her again. She stood in front of my face and didn't blink for what felt like minutes. The air was still while she stared at me. But she suddenly hugged me and told me to go upstairs to the west room and rest.

I heard her on the phone talking to her sister, my great-aunt Almo, but couldn't make out all the words. I could hear better if I cracked the door. The conversation floated from the kitchen, around the dining room, and drifted upstairs. She was crying. When Edna hung up the phone, she came upstairs, dry-eyed. She sat on the side of the bed and held my hand.

"Sometimes, things happen to a girl. God loves you and will protect you if you believe in him. From him, you will receive strength. You are already a strong girl, just like my sisters and me, and you will survive."

Then she looked at me in silence. I believed her. I felt my inner strength grow as I learned to stand up for myself and my wobbly middle school legs got stronger.

My tears dried as I finally saw a glimmer of the circle of God and nodded.

Sixteen

A Thief

Back home and at school, dunked, touched, and defeated, I failed to charm random shoppers into buying cans of peanuts. A very sweaty, too tall for my uniform, Blue Bird, I was assigned to a spot in front of the drug store. The prize for selling a record-breaking ton of cocktail nuts was not only a badge, but a "fly up" to Campfire Girls.

The sun cruelly threw heat over my station on the sidewalk while I squinted, dreading the duty. I didn't feel rejected when people smiled and kept walking because who'd buy them anyway? Peanut butter, brittle, salted, unsalted were not my favorite. The cardboard cases beside the card table held endless cans of nuts. Looking for words on the can to add to my pitch, it was no use. I was joyless.

Imagine how easy the Girl Scout cookie sales pitch would be, "If you love Coconut and Chocolate, this is the cookie for you." Or, "A Thin Mint is the perfect sweet note after dinner." Or, "Place a dish of a variety of cookies out at your next party, and you'll be a hit."

On peanuts, "Place a dish of peanuts out on the bar just like the bowling alley, and your guests will feel at home." Maybe being stationed in front of the bowling alley would be better.

"Hello, Janet. How are you this fine day?"

I was startled out of my daydream. I squinted up into the sun, and a smiling neighbor, who probably never set foot in a bowling alley, bought six cans bringing the total for the day to over $20.00! Whew! I'd made progress, and I could relax.

The next Blue Bird arrived early. Her father moved my last case of peanuts aside with his foot as he opened and stacked her boxes. She said in a voice laced with superiority, "Oh, look, you still have one case left."

I quietly hoped she'd trip.

After my shift, I went into the drug store, washed my hands, and checked the cash envelope in my pocket. It was somehow thrilling to see so many bills. I looked for a good place to write all the sales information outside the envelope when I saw it — a bow and arrow set.

I picked up the package, looked at the price, and took the money out of the envelope. I walked to the counter and made the purchase, counted the change and the remaining cash, rounded up the total, and pocketed the extra coin.

As I walked out of the store, planning to practice in the backyard, I wondered if there was a badge I could win at camp.

A couple of things happened at the same time.

There was a voice, no, more like a feeling. I looked up and turned around, looking for the speaker. I'd stolen something and got caught. I didn't see anyone, and as my heart pounded out of my chest, I knew I had to go back in. I felt a push as light as a butterfly wing and smelled doughnuts. I walked back into the store. I looked right and left, waiting for the police to pounce.

The resolute walk to the counter was slow motion. My body felt like lead on my way toward certain damnation. I stood at the counter like the condemned and confessed.

I told the cashier that I had to return the bow and arrow. Before I finished my statement, the door opened, and sunlight washed over the counter. Dad stood silhouetted in the bright sun, outlined in the entrance, and asked loudly, "What the heck are you doing inside the store?"

I stammered, "I'll be right out."

I knew I had to tell the truth. Pulling up some strength, I fast-talked my confession at the cashier, "I thought I could buy this. I really wanted it, but I took the money from my Campfire Peanut sales."

I knew God was watching this — nothing was as important as catching a thief, and I was a thief. The man just looked at me. He waited until I nearly fainted and then said, "Thank you, young lady. I'll take two cans of peanuts."

My father walked in and started to take it further, but the man behind the counter just looked at him and gave him a guy nod. I was glad; it gave my dad a minute to collect himself.

I replaced the cash and brought in two cans of peanuts. The clerk shook my hand and declared me an honest kid. I wasn't, really.

Dad loaded the last box of cans into the trunk and said, "All my poker buddies are buying your last case. Get in the car, young lady."

Faced with the appalling sin of thievery, I wrote a letter to God and requested a guardian angel. I wrote my promise to live an honest life, and since I didn't have a brother, I added I needed help. Tucked under my pillow, I checked it every night and every morning, and it was there.

I was busy getting ready for church on Sunday, resigned to being Presbyterian, and decided to check under the pillow after church.

It was gone. My mother must have taken it, but she denied it. Dad acted like he didn't know what I was talking about. It was gone, and I knew they took it, but just in case, I thanked God for the favor and added thanks, just in case I had a guardian angel.

Seventeen

The Shooter

"It's time you learned to shoot."

"Shoot what?" My question was moody and silent.

"Are you ready or not?" My grandfather Earl Shryer could read my face, a surprising skill since I felt invisible.

We stood on the dirt and gravel drive facing the barn at The Ranch. It was the same place where we cleaned horse's feet, washed their sweet, sweaty bodies, and curried them after riding. I had serious one-on-one girl-horse conversations with carrots in my pocket.

Nailed to the rickety, drab wooden doors was a large hand-painted circular target. In my hand was an old pistol that I imagined my grandfather used to blast birds away from my grandmother's garden. It was clean, oiled, heavy, and unwieldy.

In a deep, serious, 'this is the truth that needs to be told' voice, my grandfather said, "We don't have a boy, so you need to learn."

Seriously? I couldn't believe this is what I meant when I said to God I'd live a good life. I tried to remember every move, every thought, and feeling, every word, the smell of orange blossoms wafting on the breeze over the drive. I muttered to myself, "When I get home . . . " I pictured Annette and me sitting in her living room listening to Elvis Presley on the record player while her mom made root beer floats. They'd laugh about shooting lessons. That would put life back into perspective.

Standing with my grandfather in front of the barn door, he talked, giving me instructions. He woke me out of my daydream when he placed the pistol in my hands. He pointed at the target on the side of the barn. I closed one eye, took a deep breath, and squeezed the trigger. Grandfather, with his hat tilted back on his brow and a hand over his eyes, said with a straight face and a smirk, "We have some work to do."

My fate was sealed. My new life skill was killing with a gun. Not a drowning gunny sack filled with squirming kittens or yipping new-born puppies, not a baseball bat for poor blind hissing possums, not an ax for flapping, panicked chickens, but a gun. I felt sick and wished my brother had lived. He could do the shooting and kill things. I could talk with the hens in the brooding hutch. I would sweetly lie that they had nothing to worry about as they clucked and pecked around me.

Nothing made Grandfather mad except democrats and jackrabbits. I didn't share what I was learning about my mother, who promoted "socialist" theory. My Shryer grandparents had an opinion of my mother — she was trouble.

The shooting lessons had a purpose. My grandfather's master plan included his tractor, a very old, heavy, dirty, solid piece of equipment with directional push/pull levers and pedals. Every day he'd drive the quadrants of his twenty-three acres of orange trees and make notes in his little pocket book about irrigation, weeds, pests, and the number of jackrabbits he saw.

I had to shoot every day until I could hit the middle circle of the target on the barn door. I practiced and got the center almost every time. He was right; it took work.

The flaw was that he really and truly expected me to shoot and kill jackrabbits from my seated perch on the back of his bumpy tractor. It was ridiculous in the extreme!

I hoped it would work the same way it worked in the bloodless story my father told. He'd come home on leave after basic training in 1941 and was walking through the groves contemplating his future in the South Pacific War. He came face to face with a jackrabbit. They stared at each other for a second. Then dad raised his hand, pointed his finger, and yelled, "Bang!" and the rabbit fell over, dead.

Sitting on the rear tractor bench, the smell of oily smoke drifting over me, I watched — ready for the moment, practicing using predatory eyes, down each row of orange trees. I did wish for a magical rabbit mind trick that would alert them long before the sound and smell of this machine came near. I was the murderer on watch, the one who kills: me — the bloodthirsty monster. I had a job. Maybe someone else would be happy waiting for the sharp report of the gun and the sight of a vaporized rabbit exploding with the force of the bullet, but not me.

If I'd taken it more seriously, rather than letting my eyesight blur with tears, pray with all my heart they would run, and miss every one of them on purpose, I might have turned out different and better. Maybe I wouldn't have to be strong because "things can happen to girls." Maybe I would've been more like a boy who could shoot.

When my grandfather was near the end of his life, I drove up the state to pick up my Dad and visited Earl in the hospital in Tulare, CA. We talked about small things, updates, and great-granddaughters. Then my grandfather took a deep laborious breath as if he was preparing for something to say. We waited as he said in his deep voice, "Janet, you are the sweetest girl in the world, but you're the world's worst shot."

My dad thought it was funny. To me, it was one of those "truth" statements acknowledging the lack of a boy, like the news I couldn't get up on toe shoes because I didn't have the right feet or tendons, kind of too bad for you . . . from the man I admired the most. I kissed him on his forehead, told him the truth, I loved him. I thanked him for all the good times we had, the horse rides, and grumbling about Democrats and . . . the wild and free jackrabbits. His eyes lit up, and he chuckled. He was one of my best friends, one who loved me, one who protected and forgave. Those are the last laughs we shared. My grandfather died in April 1976. I was 29.

Eighteen

Inside the Dance

The light flipped on, and Dad came quietly into my room in the early morning dark.

"Get out of bed and get dressed as fast as you can," he said in a quiet voice.

I knew the standard routine, and in minutes I was dressed. My light blue suitcase was packed with emergency clothes and the items needed to travel fast. As I moved silently into the living room, my father came out of their bedroom and said in a low voice, "I have a box and a blanket for the kittens."

I followed him back into my room and opened the closet door. Gypsy looked at me and mewed, the small ones sleeping like furry balls between her legs. My father came close and quietly said, "Put the kittens in first, and Gypsy will follow."

I moved with purpose, gently scooping up kittens one by one, putting them carefully in the box. The kittens mewed until their mother gracefully climbed into the box and gave them reassuring licks. My Gypsy looked up; we both knew what was going on. I carried the box onto the back porch where Dad had set up food, water, and a sandbox.

Few words were ever spoken while this performance of the "emergency ballet" moved silently forward.

Dad handed me the house keys and disappeared back down the hall as my parents carefully moved out of the bedroom, my mom's body, wrapped in a blanket, limply draped over Dad's shoulder. I opened the front door for them to walk through and down the steps. She moaned as they walked to the car. I locked the front door, checked it, and then followed them down the front steps. I looked through the car window at Mom, snugly wrapped on the back seat, and got in front with Dad.

"Drive slowly," Mom gasped in a small voice, too loud for her severe migraines, which often sent her to the hospital.

"Don't worry, sweetheart," Dad said with loving kindness. "We'll get there safely."

I knew better than to say anything and wondered which family would take me in for the night. Would I know them, or were they dreaded strangers? When he dropped me off at a stranger's house, I never knew what to expect. Would I sleep on a couch, on the floor, or worse, with a person I didn't know? It would only be a year or two before they could leave me home and go to the hospital without me in the middle of the night. I kept to myself as the car sped through the sleeping town.

We came to a street of houses I didn't recognize, and Dad pulled up to a house with a porch light on. It was a tidy one-story, ranch-style house on a street with large trees and expansive green lawns. A woman, a total stranger in a bathrobe, stepped into the light. So this is where I was going to spend the rest of the night. A shiver moved through my silent body as my dad reached over me to open the passenger door. He said in a low voice, "Don't forget to say thank you."

I nodded and got out of the car glancing into the back seat through the window. I knew the routine. I looked at Mom; we blew silent kisses to each other as my dad rounded the back of the car with my suitcase. She put her hand over her mouth and wept as we walked away. I knew better than to show sadness or fear. This pain was my mother's, and my part was to show strength whether or not I felt it. It was my job to reassure my parents that this choice of the drop off was a good choice. My heart was squeezing, and I felt relieved as Dad and the smiling lady urged me to come into her house. No problem, easy . . . as the words to a creepy but familiar poem danced around my cynical mind:

"Will you walk into my parlor?" said a spider to a fly;
"'Tis the prettiest little parlor that ever you did spy."

Dad, still holding onto the blue suitcase, urgently communicated the tightly scripted plans to the smiling woman. I was not enthused.

1) "I don't know when I'll be back."

2) "I'll call when I know."

3) "I'll try to get back in time to take her to school."

The "*Spider*" lady said, "Oh, don't worry, we'll be fine." Then she turned to me and said sweetly, "Won't we?"

"Oh no, no!" said the little fly, "for I've often heard, who goes up your winding stair can ne'er come down again."

I knew my part in the dance. I'd performed this routine plenty of times — smile with acceptance, be quiet, then smile reassuring-ly in Dad's direction. When I was little, being taken out of bed and dropped at a stranger's house terrified me. Now I was stronger and could protect myself.

The lady introduced me to a tall frowning man in a plaid bathrobe who stood with his arms crossed. I tensed instinctively and stayed quiet as he said in a not-so-happy voice, turning away from us to go back where he came from, "It's late — let's get to bed."

She put her arm around me, and we moved quickly down the hall. She pointed to the bathroom before we stopped at a closed door. The lady leaned into my ear and quietly said, "This is the bathroom. You'll be staying in the playroom on the other side of the boy's room."

Other side of what? I didn't understand the setup but didn't ask anything. I looked up at the lady while she quietly opened the door and said with her finger to her lips, "sh-h-h-h, the boys are asleep."

This was unbelievable. I followed her into the quiet room. She closed the door and tiptoed quietly past two lumps of boys in their twin beds. The lady opened a door on the opposite side to the play-room. Glancing back, I thought about getting to the bathroom, then gave it up and tiptoed through the open playroom door.

A small bed was neat and made up with clean towels folded at the foot of the bed. The lady pointed to a little glass of water on a table next to the bed and mouthed, "Sleep tight. See you for breakfast." She turned and re-entered her son's bedroom.

I was alone and felt confined with a bathroom that could be reached only through the boy's room. Ugh.

I changed my clothes and skipped brushing my furry teeth. It was too much trouble to get to and from the bathroom in the dark. I sighed as I sat on the bed and looked around the room again, this time more carefully. I looked at windows and doors and what not to bump into. I noted places to hide just in case and the best path to leave if it was necessary. I saw a door different from the one to the boy's room. My heart beating loudly, I got off the bed to explore. The back door to the playroom led to a patio, then to a flower bed and a lawn. On the right was a paved sidewalk to the garage. I felt I had a good picture and was too tired to go any further. Satisfied with my options, I went to bed.

It was still dark when I woke, having to go to the bathroom. I moaned and tried to talk my body out of having to go, dreading what I had to do. I put on my slippers and bathrobe and went outside. I made a choice. Relieved, I hurried back to my bed, kicked off my slippers, and fell fast asleep.

Boy voices woke me up, and I opened my eyes to see one boy about my age and one younger, standing by the bed. They said at the same time, talking over each other, "Hey, there's mud on your slippers. Where did you go last night? Did you sleepwalk?"

I sat up in bed and pulled my bathrobe over my shoulders, and looked at them, eye to eye, "Guess so."

There was no way I was going to admit to using the garden. The lady called for the boys to leave me alone and come to the kitchen. The boys stared at me like I was a bug then ran out of the playroom.

I got dressed, made the bed, arranged the towels, put my dirty slippers in my suitcase, closed it, picked it up, walked through the boy's room, and put it at the front door. I used the real bathroom and brushed my teeth. The lady called everyone to breakfast, and I walked toward the lady's voice. The boys watched my every move as I seated myself at the table. I was pretty numb and wanted to get through this day without harm or loss. I was silent as I picked up my napkin. As I moved in for a bite of toast, the father said, looking over his morning paper, "Sleep well, young lady?"

My throat closed, and I put the toast down. The boys started to jab-ber, talking over each other, "She sleepwalked." "Her slippers were muddy." "Yeah, and then . . . "

I stared at them, barely breathing or blinking. I never broke my stare, and the boys abruptly stopped talking. They just looked at their plates as their parents laughed at the absurd idea that their guest sleepwalked. I was silent. Thankfully, the morning progressed with the boys staying far away from me, the bug girl.

I sat in the living room, waiting for my dad. I watched the family go through the motions of getting ready for work and school and waited. The phone rang, and I heard the lady say, "She was lovely, and we'd be happy to have her stay with us any time."

"*Never!*" I thought to myself.

I wanted out, done with this routine. I wanted to go home or school where life could be normal; I wanted to play with Gypsy and her kittens.

The lady came into the living room and said in a sweet voice, "Your father will be here shortly. Why don't you come into the kitchen with me?"

I watched the two boys through the front window as they got into the car with their father. They both turned and looked at me one last time. I turned away from their stare and slowly followed the lady into the kitchen and sat in a chair. I listened to her chatter about how nice it was to have a girl for a while and how she'd love to have me back again and maybe we could go shopping. She tried to be kind and understanding, and I'm certain I was more polite in my words than the sarcastic conversation in my head.

I looked over my shoulder, through the window where my dad would park, as the lady talked, pausing to laugh at her own silliness.

As I finally walked to the car carrying the emergency blue suit-case, Dad talked and asked questions about my stay. As I listened and added a few polite bits to the conversation, I realized I didn't know any of their names.

∼✑∽

Trust was not and is not easy for me. I've found myself still checking pathways from a bed to a door when I stay with a friend. I am not comfortable "crashing" or sleeping in a place I can't control. I automatically track, check, and test. The places I had to stay whenever the choreography of the midnight dance meant dropping me off at a stranger's home taught me to be cautious and careful like the spider in the poem. When the choreography of the midnight dance began and I ended up at a stranger's home, I may have looked polite and ladylike, but the tempest inside ran to its own beat, like the wings of a fly. In the last stanza of Mary Howitt's 1829 poem:

> And now, dear little children, who may this story read,
> To idle, silly, flattering words, I pray you ne'er give heed:
> Unto an evil counselor, close heart, and ear, and eye,
> And take a lesson from this tale of the Spider and the Fly."

Nineteen

Cops, Camp Fire Girls, and a Mummy Bag

Girls leaned out the windows of the waiting bus and laughed as I struggled with my sleeping bag. I tried not to cry, but tears are pushy, especially when the girls laughed at me and my stupid bag.

When a peanut-selling Blue Bird "flies up," she becomes a Camp Fire Girl. I had achieved something new, like the marching band, and I felt some confidence. My parents warned me to be careful because I wasn't old enough to make life choices. I heard it but through a filter of rebellious self-determination. I knew camping and could bring my camping history to these two weeks of character building, spine strengthening, badge earning experiences.

We finished the first week, and we were preparing to move sites. Every Camp Fire Girl had to know how to break camp, secure a sleeping bag, and load up. This morning started with our assigned duties. Mine was to clean up the campfire, erase our presence, and return it to nature. I finished on time. I not only completed on time, but I also got a high mark.

I was doing my best to roll my ridiculous sleeping bag with a piece of rope. This wasn't a regular sleeping bag. I had my dad's WWII "mummy" bag. My parents argued it was cost-effective, and since they had the old, moldy, dusty thing stored in the garage, there was no need to buy a new one. I was in junior high school, a new teenage girl with some confidence, worry, and concern. Most girls our age had all that too, but without a smelly, dusty mummy bag added to the mix.

The original purpose of this thing was to hold a tall soldier tight when zipped up. This bag had a rusty zipper. Once it was zipped up, it was impossible to zip down. If it was down, it was impossible to zip up. There was no lining or filling, just a single, smelly, heavy, green fabric shell. Soldiers slept in their clothes, but my mother added a sheet, blanket, and pillow for comfort. Since those comforts were not attached to the shell, they bunched in all the wrong spots and became impossible for a skinny 13-year-old to roll and tie. The rope was fine when the bag was rolled tight by my giant father, but I could not manage this monster. It was a nightmare.

Finally, a teenage counselor jumped out of the bus and came to my rescue. He was not kind. He was there to teach camping skills and show no soft compassion in front of a bunch of teenage girls. He did see the problem and told me he'd help me roll for the rest of the week so we wouldn't be late every day. I wanted to melt into the ground. I glanced over my shoulder to reaffirm my excellent campfire clean-up and get a tiny piece of confidence.

On the bus and singing our camp songs at the top of our lungs, we arrived at our next camping adventure. We learned to pitch a tent, fry an egg on a hot rock, get into and out of a canoe, paddle across the lake, learn survival techniques, march in a straight line, and other critical camping skills. We sang songs, learned to track, identify, and log bird sightings. It was fun being with a bunch of girls camping, and we earned badges for our assignments. It was important to earn badges because moving up to become an Indian Princess depended on how many badges you won and for what. I focused on becoming an Indian Princess and hoped it didn't depend on sleeping bag rolling and tying.

The camp counselor did help with the bag, and before we loaded up to go home, he took me aside, "Please tell your parents to get the right kind of bag before next summer."

I said yes, of course.

"You didn't learn a thing about getting ready to hit the trail after breaking camp, and you will not get a badge." He was a little nasty with his teen-counselor power.

Ugh, I knew it and simply nodded.

As the hot August afternoon sun danced through the pine shadows randomly cast onto the dry mountain road, our yellow school bus rumbled down the Rim of the World, State Highway 38, to join Interstate 10 on its way to Campfire Headquarters in Pomona, California. We Campfire Girls hung on, loving the seat-belt free ride. The counselors called for quiet and after settling down finally called for camp songs. Our bus filled with 99 *Bottles of Beer on The Wall*, laughter, and stories about the two-week camping experience.

Oh, how I steamed about my parents and the stupid ideas that made my life hard. My new friends, gained from our shared camping experience, gave me advice as we rode the bus down the mountain. Tammy piped up, "I think you should cry and tell them how hard it was for you. My dad would feel sorry for me." Sounds easy.

Patty added, "No, I think you should be careful and calmly explain you missed a badge because of the bag." Hmm, that one might be smarter.

Diane, the joker, said, "I think you should throw it away and say a bear ate it." This would be for parents who hadn't met Mary, the bear, the very bear that ripped our campsite to pieces in Yellowstone.

❧

The return agreement was clear. The girls would be dropped off at the Camp Fire Office in downtown Pomona. Parents were instructed to sign the sheet on the outside wall, confirming the correct child was picked up. We stood around, talking and laughing, while one by one, cars drove up to collect a girl or two. The last girl was picked up and waved goodbye. I was sure my parents were working and might be late. I gave them grace. I sat on the steps and pulled out my Camp Fire Girl badge book. The afternoon got cooler as the sun set behind the building, and looking around, I noticed the streetlights came on. I began to worry.

It got darker and I started to wonder how long it would take to walk home with my duffle and monster sleeping bag. Just when I was considering how I would haul my heavy load, a police car drove up and stopped. The policeman got out and walked up to me and asked, "Are you waiting for your parents?"

Why did tears want to burst out? I wasn't frightened. I was mad. I was old enough to see my part in this family, and frankly, my parents were not playing their part very well.

"I've been waiting since we got here at about four o'clock."

He said, "It's nearly nine."

I was a little shocked by the passage of time but didn't overreact.

"I need to call them, but I don't know where the nearest phone is. Can you show me?"

"We'll call from my car. Give me your gear, and I'll get you home."

I was conflicted. They didn't give me a key because they didn't want it lost in the camping process. I didn't want to sit on the steps of my house in the dark if they weren't home. The policeman asked for our phone number. He got on his radio and asked the station to call my home. The phone rang and rang — no answer.

"I'll have to take you to the station until we get a hold of your parents."

I agreed — it felt safer than being left at my house. As we started to drive away, my dad's car skidded into the parking area. Out of breath, my dad got out of our car and ran over to the police car.

"Sir, are you this girl's father?"

The policeman stood tall, though my father loomed over him. My father, with his eye on the policeman, directed his voice to him and to me.

"Yes. Janet, get out of the . . . "

The policeman interrupted my father and said with even more authority, "Young lady, stay where you are. And sir, please stay where you are."

My father froze.

The policeman looked at him with no emotion and said, "Driver's license, please."

My father fumbled to pull it out of his wallet. The headlights of our car lit our gathering as the night got darker. I was so excited to see an authority figure speak to my father like that. The WWII mummy sleeping bag, the forgotten daughter — I wanted him arrested.

"Is this your father?"

The policeman handed me the driver's license. I took it from his hand and looked at it as long as I could just to make him squirm.

"Janet Cathryn!" my father yelled.

The policeman knew what I was doing, and he, with his back to my father, smiled and nodded, ending my torturous act.

"Yes, he's my father," I said to the officer, solemn, accusing, and judgmental.

"Get in the car, young lady," my father fumed.

My father tried to regain some authority, and I moved as slowly as I could. I thanked the policeman, and he tipped his hat, got in his car, and drove away.

On our drive home, my father decided to take the path of "it's not our fault, we are busy professionals, and it's not easy to remember everything."

That was probably a defining moment. I knew my father was the worst problem solver, the worst decision maker ever. I tuned him out as we drove up the drive and piled my stuff out of the car onto the front yard.

"I had to have a camp counselor help with my sleeping bag every night because it's impossible to roll and secure."

I could see my father's reply starting to form, and I jumped in, "I didn't get a badge because of it. And the counselor said to never bring this bag back to camp again."

My father fumed, picked up the tied mummy bag, threw the rope aside, emptied the sheet, blanket, and pillow onto the lawn, and threw the bag in the trash with a loud soundtrack of frustration.

"There, are you satisfied?"

He asked as if he was talking to someone thirty years old. I knew he felt guilty but I was not his friend or co-worker. He was a parent. I was his daughter. He could not possibly distinguish who I was in this angry conversation.

I went into my room and got ready for a bath. Exhaustion swept over me as hot water filled the tub. We had one bathroom, and I didn't care if anyone else needed to use it. While I soaked and washed my hair, I heard my mother come home. I heard her ask where I was as she put her keys in the hallway dish. She knocked and came in. Sitting on the toilet seat, she looked a bit confused.

She asked, "Why are you in the bath so late? Didn't you get back this afternoon?"

The questions were left open as I washed, dunked, and got ready to get out to dry off.

I finally said, "Ask Dad."

Her face changed with a dawning thought, "I'll be back. Take your time, sweetheart."

I took my time, remembering skin cream, and heard rising voices fill the house as my father got my mother's fury.

She came back into the bathroom. "You had to wait until dark?"

She looked at me like she'd just heard I was tied up and tortured. I nodded, wrapped a towel around my body, and started to comb out my wet hair.

"What happened, my god? What happened?"

Her voice escalated to the level of outrage. I had a feeling it was time to come out with the story, but I had to be careful. Alliances shift, and I wanted her on my side.

"We got back to the Camp Fire Headquarters, and Dad didn't show up until the police found me on the steps."

I wasn't sure she heard about the police — as her eyebrows shot up, her dark pink colored lips opened, her eyes got big, and she said, "What police?" Her voice rose to a deeply powered voice, "DAMN IT, Loren, what did you do this time?"

She got up in slow motion, then flying out of the bathroom, she stormed into the living room. I brushed my teeth while the argument got bigger and louder. I cleaned up, erased my presence just like I learned at camp, and moved to get into bed with a book and Gypsy. My parents continued to argue about who was at fault, though there was no question that it was my father who forgot to pick me up.

I thought about my new skills, getting in and out of a canoe, frying an egg on a hot rock, tracking beasts, logging bird sightings, manipulating my parents, and wondered if this Camp Fire thing was for me, after all. I think it was.

Twenty

Showdown in Vegas

Las Vegas 1960

"What do you mean that our teenage daughter has to sit in a children's room?" said my mother, standing tall, her hand on her hip, looking elegant, sounding lofty. She towered over a short, stout man who stood as tall as he could at the door from the lobby into the dining room of an Italian restaurant. We went to this restaurant my dad heard about after a particularly grueling Las Vegas gun show at the Stardust Hotel in Las Vegas.

Shabby is pretty close to the description of this little spot. It was decorated with plastic grapes wound through strings of lights. The wallpaper was deep red flocked, and the pictures on the wall were travel posters of Italy. The lobby was lined with banquet chairs and had two slot machines in the corner near the door. People were waiting to be taken into the restaurant. They watched my mother.

The man had a tie knotted so tight it made his face red and puffy. He spoke, looking up to my lofty mother in his raspy strangled voice, "Those are the rules, and that's final. Children under 18 cannot wait in the casino area."

I was a young teenager, and all I wanted to do was sit and read. But management had a children's room upstairs for everyone under 18.

Dad, a fanatic collector of Civil and Revolutionary War gun reproductions, dragged my mom and me to gun shows. We'd traveled to Las Vegas to visit Hoover Dam and the Paiute Indian Reservation while dad looked at guns. Mom took charge of the history lessons, and though I could be moody, she had a way of interesting me in the most detailed historical facts. After our tour, we went back to The Stardust to meet Dad for dinner.

There was little for Mom and me to do at a gun show. My father mused over ancient fighting weapons and got all wrapped up in lengthy conversations with gun lovers. While we waited for him, Mom and I took our own time walking the aisles of weaponry.

"Oh, look at this!" she said. I turned around and saw her pointing at a small cannon. She walked over to the booth and got the pot bellied man's attention. Removing the toothpick he was chewing, he mangled, "Hello Ma'am, I mean Miss, how can I help you?"

"How much is this?" She pointed at the cannon then, with half-closed eyes, raised her eyebrows and gave the man a look of pure, honest interest.

He quickly thumbed through his pricing manual, and before he could speak, she said, "What kind of, uh, oh I don't know, bullets, does this contraption shoot?"

He looked momentarily stunned, gulped, and said, "It shoots balls." I thought my mother would laugh out loud, but instead, she turned her head to me. I was coughing to cover my laughter, and she cynically said, "We should buy this, point it at the Stevens, and shoot their dog's 'dump' back at them." I was stunned. Our neighbor's dog really was a problem, and my parents threatened to return the dumps he'd daily left on our front lawn.

The pot bellied man in the booth was speechless.

∾৩৲

In the discussion at the door of the restaurant, Mom took a breath. She said, in a voice you might hear in a movie, "What exactly do you expect to happen in the casino with teenage children waiting in line, with their parents, for a table in your establishment?"

The man comically drew himself up on his toes and sputtered, "We will not endanger children with corruption in our establishment." Oh boy, he had no idea what could happen in a conversation with my mother.

"Are you certain corruption will erupt while children are in line with their parents? How will you know when you see it? Does it erupt like a pimple?"

The poor man could not come up with anything to sputter other than, "IT'S THE LAW!" he sprayed spit, face to face with the Queen.

"Very well, I'll follow her, and we'll see how well you've set this up, and, if I determine," her finger pointing at the man, her fist still on her hip, "you've sidestepped in any way, I'll make sure the law pays you a visit."

My father watched. He'd gotten up and walked over to stand behind the man. His strong jaw was set, his heavy brow furrowed, and his six-foot-four body loomed over the poor guy.

The small man wielded his power like a plastic sword and told her in no uncertain terms the room upstairs was for children only, not adults. My mother, smarter than the tiny warrior, said, "That is ridiculous!"

I loved watching this back and forth between my mother and this pitiful man. She took me by the hand, and we turned to walk out. My father called out after us, deeply and theatrically, "Ina Mae, what do you want me to do?"

She said, in her queen's voice, her audience, the open-mouthed patrons, "Loren, secure the table and have that little man come find us." She spun us around, winked at me, and out we walked. She and I collapsed in laughter.

"Did you see the look on that little gargoyle's face?" she gasped.

"Oh, Mom, it was beautiful. Corruption erupting like a pimple?"

We laughed so hard, Mom and me, holding onto each other by the side of a dumpy joint in Vegas.

Dad walked out after us and said with teammate pride, "I told them all to go to hell." We howled and walked into the setting sun. We found dinner in a little café with no slot machines and recounted each minute detail of the theatrical exchange.

I suspect theatrics was the only win.

Twenty-one

Driving Lessons

"Take your foot off the damn brake, Janet. Use the clutch and downshift NOW!"

The army green, 1952 Volkswagen Beetle, hurtled brakeless down the steep, winding Mount Baldy Road. I was 16, and I had a license. This driving lesson was on the list of needed skills for me, "the girl," demanded by my father, six feet plus of urgent anger, stuffed into the passenger seat. There were no seat belts in this year of VW, and when the clutch was depressed, you could see the road through the floor.

My ears dutifully heard him, but my brain screamed "NO." Terror dried my tears, and my resolve increased. I pushed on the clutch and downshifted into second gear. As the engine growled, two parts of something screeched and then locked in as we entered another curve.

Dad bellowed, "Punch it, Janet. Stay on the inside of the curve, NOW!"

The car eased into the curve, and he yelled, "Hold the wheel and don't straighten until the straightaway."

The steering wheel shuddered. California air, scented with dry pine and dirt, buffeted noisily through the open windows. We careened down the highway, my dad shouting orders about gears and sissy driving, over the rev of the engine, and metallic squeal of the clutch.

The car was smoking and steaming; the smell of burned rubber tires wafted into the windows as we got to the bottom of the mountain and pulled into a parking lot. I was shaking as if I'd survived something deadly. Dad had the grin of conquest — a brigadier general proud of his nearly dead troops.

He had me drive to the ice cream parlor for banana splits, the typical celebration to make it all better. The driving lesson was a great success. That's what he called it. I called it something else as my shaking hands managed to scoop into the dripping, fudge-covered ice cream.

Dad believed a car needed to be broken in, like a horse. He believed using brakes was a sign of poor driving skills. He believed making the light was a matter of acceleration. He believed he was the best driver in the world.

I believed he was dangerous. I believed he was not trustworthy.

I believed I could not be trusted because . . .

Driving home from church in 1962, from behind the steering wheel of my grandparent's 4-door sedan, I opened my eyes to swirling dust, smoke, blood, steaming twisted metal, and the far-off sound of a horn.

∿

I was 14 and two summers into my training behind the levers of the tractor and metal steering wheel of the flat-bed truck. On The Ranch, I drove with confidence under my grandfather Earl's teaching. He was strong and direct, not loud like dad. He went over everything I needed to learn before I drove the tractor for the first time. The clutch/gear on the flat-bed truck was my favorite. I loved the orderly sequential function of those two actions and the effort it took to make it happen just right. That day in 1962, my grandfather continued my driving lessons in the 4-door sedan on the way home from church. He had a clear vision of what was needed to turn me into a useful farmhand.

The day dawned as one of those unique, beautiful Central Valley days. Bright, clear blue sky presided over the second corn crop of the season. The stalks were deep green, ready to be harvested, heavy with sweet cobs you could almost smell. Church finished, and as usual, I was lifted by inspiration and joy in the closing hymn. This church had the best, most enthusiastic, loudest singers of all the churches I attended. The organist was a little short for the setup, but she let nothing get between her size and the music. I related my clutch gear struggle to hers. She threw her body into the organ and almost had to stand to reach the complex set of pedals. At the same time, she pushed and pulled buttons and pulleys to get the best sound out of the organ. I let myself ride the music and the voices of the congregation to the top of the peaked roof of the sanctuary. I thought God might be very happy with this crowd of well-dressed faithful people.

It wasn't quite hot, but it was warm enough to open the car windows. My grandparents, Earl and Edna Shryer, proudly invited me to drive. Grandma sat in the front seat, and Grandpa, leaning over the back seat, gave play-by-play directions as we eased out of the church parking lot. Ease back, check your mirrors, and start slowly. Backing out, I remember feeling his pride wash over me. Other church members waved their support of the young one being taught the necessary skills. He was easing me into near adulthood with trust and love.

Driving home, we negotiated every turn, stop, and arm signal. As we neared the drive, he gently instructed me to slow down enough to make the right turn onto the gravel road to the farmhouse. At a little too high a speed, my foot was a little too hard on the brake, the wheels locked in the turn, and the car started to spin and skid in the rocky dirt as I pressed the brake to stop. A concrete irrigation column on the edge of the drive rose twelve feet high. As the spin turned us faster and faster to the right, the car moved in a circle. At some point in the turn, we crashed into the column.

My grandfather hadn't taught me how to manage a spinning, out of control, 3500-pound piece of machinery.

Things seemed to happen in slow motion inside the car, a sudden smash of breaking glass, the thud and grunt of heads and bodies being flung from front to back and side to side. In the abrupt halt of motion, rising steam, the smell of burning oil, battery acid, and urine filled the twisted space.

Soft groans floated from the backseat where my grandfather lay twisted on the floor behind me and from the front where my grandmother wept in a crumpled heap. I turned my head to see something on my left, my head on the horn on the steering column. In the clear, bright summer Sunday morning, the stream of sound faded as I lost consciousness. Years later, as we chatted over tea, Aunt Thelma told me what happened next.

"The dog started barking, and when I went to the door to let him out, I saw a light cloud of dust moving over the grove and heard the sound of a car horn. Mother's dog ran fast out of the gate, barking down the drive. When I got to the wreck, you looked like you were sleeping, and the dog jumped on mother's lap, trying to lick her face. She didn't move, and I took the struggling dog off her body. I had to run back to the house to call for an ambulance, and while I ran, I remembered I hadn't seen my father. I was about to run back, but I was the only one to call, so I kept going. I remember seeing you and thinking it was good you were asleep."

I wasn't sleeping. I'd been knocked out cold.

When the ambulance came, I tried to get out of the car with the help of someone, maybe a policeman. I saw people move my grandparents into the ambulance with stretchers, and I collapsed, blood running down my face, sobbing in the dirt and gravel of the drive. The ambulance drove away, and as the sound of the siren faded, I knew. I knew I had killed my grandparents.

A policeman took me to the same hospital where I was born, and my grandparents lay gravely damaged. He told me to rest. I asked a nurse about my grandparents and was told they were doing what they could.

"My head hurts, and I'm bleeding," I called after her.

"Don't worry, kid, it's nothing." She raised her voice as she turned her head and rushed away.

I was 14. I knew when I was being ignored. I wept myself into sleep, alone, bloody, repeating the prayer ". . . if I should die before I wake . . . " I didn't expect any god to care. I knew I didn't deserve to be forgiven.

I had a significant concussion and was left alone with my shock and sadness. No one questioned the well-being of a teenager in the emergency room, asleep in a chair, with blood on her head, face, and clothing. Aunt Thelma came out, found me, and yelled enough to awaken me, and called for someone to come help her niece. At that very moment the police came in. After a conversation with the hospital staff, the police saw to it that I was hastily re-bandaged before they took me from the emergency room, into a police car, to the station for questioning.

My aunt loudly rushed to stop them from taking me away from the hospital. She argued, she pleaded, she begged, and it was obvious she had no power. The police asked her for my father's phone number. She said he was at least four hours away. They called my father, and I hoped he'd drive like he did the day I was born.

It was too stressful for my mother to come. She was scheduled for surgery that month to fix her recurring ulcers. I wished for one of those crazy miracles — the kind where the mother suddenly sees her only daughter needs her. She would come, no matter what, but I knew her. She could not be the hero of this problem. She might be blamed, and it would make her ulcer worse. My aunt would have to fill in. She was on the phone, already yelling at the police, and the hospital, and the rulers of the universe, to stop for a moment, just a moment, and pay attention to her niece. She was my only ray of hope.

The police made me sit in a room until they were ready to question me. My face was covered in bandages, I was blind in my left eye. I had to sit in a metal chair. I shook uncontrollably and couldn't stop. I couldn't control my bladder. I hated telling them what I did, but I had to. I was in shock, and I was being treated like a criminal who peed in the chair. I was guilty. I might have thought I was lucky not to be in a holding cell, but luck was unthinkable. A policeman put a can of cola in front of me and gave me a towel to sit on. I could not imagine swallowing. I put my painful head on my arms and fell into grief. The questioning was probably quick and efficient, but it felt tricky, menacing, mean, and long.

When it was over, a policeman took me back to the hospital to wait for my father. Aunt Thelma met us at the entrance, grabbing me into her arms as she shot venomous looks at the policeman. She sheltered me. She helped me get a shower, re-bandaged my head, and put me into some dramatically ill-fitting clean clothes from somewhere. The underpants were so huge she had to find safety pins to keep them from falling to my ankles. In the surgery waiting room, I said I wanted to sleep, and she sat by as I curled up on a couch. When I woke up with a screaming headache, she was talking with a doctor. I waited, then she told me my grandparents would live but be crippled for life. I heard, and everything broke inside me. I sobbed. Covered in blood, face swollen, headache addled, and battered, I could not hold up anymore. I broke, was admitted, sedated, and held until my father arrived.

When Dad reached us in the hospital, I still had not seen my grandparents. He took me out of the hospital, back to The Ranch, while he made some calls. The next day was a blur. I lost the sight in my left eye, and the doctor said my sight might not be harmed. No one checked my head. I slept nearly all day, and still, no one checked my head.

It was decided that I would be taken to my aunt's sister-in-law, Auntie Fae. Her ranch was close by. I stayed with Fae and her family for a couple of weeks until I could see and stay awake.

A week later, my grandparents went into surgery to repair shoulders, backs, hips, legs, and arms. At the same time, the police contacted the local district attorney. I was set to appear before a judge at the end of August, and I had to have an adult parent stand with me. The date was after my mother's operation, and my father had to stay south with Mom until the last minute.

The trial date came, and Dad arrived. He was a mess. His sadness was like a heavy coat in the hot August summer. We showed up, cleaned up by my aunts, and stood in front of the judge.

He took one look at me and asked, "Has a doctor looked at you?"

The pause was electric. I started to speak for the adults in my tribe, but Dad spoke up and said, "I have no idea."

The judge looked at me.

I said, "My aunts took care of me."

The judge, shocking all of the people in the court, said, "I order you, Mr. Shryer, to take your daughter to the hospital immediately."

I must have looked monstrous. The judge slammed his gavel and delayed my appearance.

Weeks had gone by, and I was healing, but we went to the hospital as ordered. I had a concussion, a bad one. The doctor thought I might have had a blood pool in my brain. They poked and x-rayed enough to determine the clot was dissolving, and I was not in any specific danger. I thought my father would fall apart. He sobbed and shakily asked me to forgive him. I had no capacity to process this request. I had no ability to think about everything that had happened and understand my place in it, other than being a criminal who peed in the interrogation room chair.

I eventually went to the hearing, more healed and awake, my dad by my side. The judge listened to the DA, who wanted to charge and send me to juvenile hall. The judge thought a minute or two, then said this was over and done. He didn't want to see us in his court again. I took it to mean I was not worth his time and slipped further into the deep.

My family never blamed me. My grandparents and my mother were the primary concerns, and they held me as a side concern, an innocent victim of their poor judgment. They focused on the most pressing issues of The Ranch, my grandparents, and the animals. Soon my father would have to go "down south," by which he meant LA, to care for my mother.

We went back to our family ranch, where Dad and my aunt Thelma made arrangements for the animals to be moved to other farms. Picket had died one day that summer, curled up under the shade of an orange tree in the grove. Honey Boy, our golden palomino, the rooster, and all the hens, had to be given away. My grandparents could no longer take care of the farm. Dad and Thelma made arrangements for the sidewalk to be torn out and a ramp built for wheelchairs. This sidewalk, the racetrack for Nancy, Picket, and me, was joy. I was happy. It was power. I destroyed it. I had nothing left — nothing. It was time for me to go away and remove the danger I'd become to this family. I retreated into the familiar, safe place of silence . . . my true friend.

My grandparents lived, healed, and took their new handicapped positions as ranch owners. A housekeeper and ranch hand were hired, and my father and Aunt Thelma managed the finances. Ownership was transferred 50/50 to Dad and his sister.

I listened half-heartedly to the phone conversations about yield, irrigation, frost, pickers, packing house contracts, and shipping costs. I prayed for my grandparents twice a day and gave God permission to condemn me.

My mother fussed at Dad to make tapioca pudding and heat soup for us, his two recovering girls. In between long naps, I played records and read as many books as I could find. It was my introduction to Ayn Rand. I struggled through my mother's copy of *The Fountainhead*, and I kept the book next to my bed. I took slow walks with my mom, from the bedroom, through the living room, around the coffee table, into the kitchen, and back to her bedroom.

We ate in bed, off the TV trays Dad would sweetly bring to us on his lunch break. Dad had a summer job as an engineer at a local manufacturing plant. He complained about supervising women. He said he "hated the cows." His words were "confused," "stupid," and "stubborn." I knew my mother was stronger and smarter than him. I felt included when her eyes glanced at me as if I were a co-conspirator.

"Those poor women." Mom would giggle.

We talked low, her finger tracing the crease on my forehead as she told me how my grandparents were doing. It sounded like condemnation, but she always ended with, "Darling, it wasn't your fault." Right.

ACT III

Keep Young and Beautiful

Twenty-two

The Spider and the Fly

"Said the cunning spider to the fly,
"Dear friend, what shall I do,
To prove the warm affection I've always felt for you?"

After the accident, Mom who was still recovering insisted I be tested before entering 10th grade. There was some brain damage from the concussion, and the doctor recommended they hire tutors to help me with more challenging classes in high school. Brain-damaged, bad ballet feet, piano failure, I wondered what kind of worthless lump I would be. Were my supportive grandparents blind? I was a mess, a criminal, and they championed me, even though they would live broken and in pain until they died. I wasn't worth much, so why worry if I succeeded?

That summer, my mother bravely got back on her feet after her surgery. She carried a sparkling banner of bravery, a remarkable survival in the face of certain death. She championed herself. She proposed a well thought out plan to her school, adding a dramatic plea to the school administrators for rest and a reduced teaching schedule. They fell all over themselves to make her happy.

After my birthday in August, just before school started, she took me shopping for clothes. It was, after all, my first and only entry into high school as a brain-damaged lump. I was wary but found myself wanting the attention and ease of her sparkling world. The struggle to stay detached, above center, on an edge where I could escape, collapsed. I swooned as her charm, love, and wit drew me in, inch by inch. I fell, just like a fly, into the spider's web.

She made reservations at the Tea Room in Bullock's Department Store in Pasadena, California. We sat at an elegant, finely appointed table beside the fashion runway show. I looked at the tea sandwiches and nearly wept. They were cut just like the sandwiches my mom put in my lunch bag when I was little. I struggled with what was real and did my best to stay upright and awake. It was a day straight out of an issue of Vogue Magazine. I let myself get swept into her dazzling web.

She was right there in front of me in the dressing room, so beautiful, visionary, directive, and organized. She was so sure of herself managing the sales woman like a pro, directing, reviewing, and demanding. "Oh, Miss — will you please bring us that sweet number over there, in her size, please?" "And, run to shoes for her size in these darling flats."

She chose and rejected, fussed and tucked outfit after outfit. I lost the grip I had on my soul. I rolled closer to her, started believing what she said, sure of my value, my worth, mesmerized by hope.

We came home and reviewed our day over coffee in small rose cups and saucers. She treated me like a friend, someone in common. I felt lighter. She found humor in every nook and cranny of the story. When Dad came home, he gasped at the piles of bags, boxes, and random wads of white tissue paper and demanded a fashion show. I surrendered. I let myself fall into the web of love and attention. I was hooked and blinded by her wonder, just like everyone else in her world.

I entered high school in perfect fashion. The bump on my head was now a crease, easily covered by makeup. Mom's hairdresser gave me a new hairstyle, straight out of *Seventeen*, with perfect bangs to hide the dent. I was almost convinced I had worth. I had the hair and the clothes and learned the lesson of the year. Looking good is half the battle. Stay slim and beautiful, and you'll be loved. This was a valuable lesson for this lump that crippled her grandparents.

I held my breath for a few days, those first days of high school, waiting for confidence. I was socially accepted, and no one noticed what I knew about myself. I could hide behind this stuff. I looked good, and it began to dawn on me that I had a shield. But, I needed to be smart. I told my mom that I felt better and began to pay more attention to my style. She was thrilled. She gave me advice, taught me about makeup, walking with confidence, and helped curl my hair. She eagerly pointed out that I came from a socially mediocre middle school. I had to compensate fast if I was going to rise to an acceptable level of popularity in high school. She seemed happy with me, and I felt chosen.

∽৩∾

She had a bright idea. I needed important connections, and she need-ed to help. Using her network of fan-friends, they found the most popular girls at the high school, got phone numbers and addresses, and talked with the moms. My mother set the first appointment with the unsuspecting mother of one of the most beautiful, popular girls in our class. She didn't tell me, she surprised me.

On a Saturday afternoon, she told me we had an appointment. I worried when she just smiled at my questions, but I thought we were on a new positive roll, so I gave in. We arrived at a lovely house in our town's fancy neighborhood. She turned to me, sort of bouncy, and said, "We're meeting with Mrs. Taylor. Her daughter is also new to your school, and we think you'll be great friends."

I lost my breath. I didn't know how to stop this disastrous thing. I was innocent and did nothing wrong. This horror was not deserved. I suddenly understood what the condemned felt facing a firing squad.

Sandy Taylor was a sweet girl, and she avoided me like the plague. She was the most popular, most beautiful, best dressed, most grace-ful, and coolest girl in school. When she arrived on our campus, everyone stopped breathing. Boys lost their minds, and girls sud-denly knew they had no idea who they were on the scale of Sandy. She and her group floated like models through sophomore year. They had grace, money, and the starvation diets that go along with fame. My mother, using her charm and power, tricked Sandy's poor mother into meeting with us. Mom concocted this manic scene and convinced this unfortunate victim, I was just like her daughter. I was not!

We waited in Mrs. Taylor's beautifully decorated living room with tea and cookies. I was stunned. Sandy's mother twittered and fussed around my mother, making sure everything was picture perfect. Sandy never appeared. Her mother knocked on her door, and Sandy whimpered she had a headache. Her mom made compelling, kind excuses for her girl. I wanted to slip a note under the door saying that it was all a weird mistake, we were at the wrong house, and my mother was crazy. The insane scene played out politely. My mother rose, exerting her persuasive personality. She cleverly let Sandy's mom think it was her fault, and we left.

I was humiliated, furious, and resolved. On my walks to and from high school, I'd talk to God. I told him I was not going to let my mother run my life and needed his help. I had to be careful, so would he let me know if I was foolish? I had a fleeting cautionary thought about just being me talking to God. Maybe I was on some list, a failure list with waning hope.

One day after school, the phone rang.

"Hello?" I said, making an off-handed attempt to sound adult, annoyed that I had to take a message. I expected to hear the voice of the electric or a loan company calling to remind my father to pay the past-due bill. I wanted the lights on when I got home from school.

"Mrs. Shryer, this is Pomona High School, and we're calling about Janet."

My throat got a little dry, and my heart fluttered. Without missing a beat, in my mother's voice, I said, "Yes?"

"Well, Janet signed up for Chemistry for next year, and we are not confident she's prepared for the difficulty of the classwork."

My mind raced, and suddenly, I became the mother I needed. In her voice, I said, "Oh, really? Well, I am equally confident she is more than prepared. Please enroll her in the class."

I hung up. My ears were ringing, my heart pounded. Sweat beads slinked down my neck into my blouse. I lied. I made a choice without discussion, correction, or judgment. I flexed my tenth grade muscle.

A new voice arose out of the rubble of childhood. True, my confidence and trust ebbed and flowed as I got older, but while I tested the new and exciting boundaries of my own decision making, I didn't share my worries or concerns with my mother. I cheered her on, kept up my style, dieted, and kept my mouth shut.

During the year, I auditioned and tried out for teams, quit the band, made the speech and debate team, tried out for the rally squad, and signed up for college prep classes, including Chemistry. When I shared the class and activities list for junior year with my parents, my mother said, "My dear, are you sure about this?"

I assured her, "It's no big deal." I held my breath, dreading being caught for lying, and waited. She said, lowering her papers, "Oh, I'm sure it's not, my darling." She lost interest, took up the chat with Dad about her successful return to teaching and her new performance schedule.

One brilliant spring afternoon, as I walked from rally tryouts to lunch, I saw a girl sitting on the grassy hill beside the gym. I walked over and sat next to her. I asked, "Are you new?" Her green eyes and curly red hair were so cute, I felt happy.

She grinned and laughed, "Yep."

We became best friends. When I told her the Sandy story, she laughed until she cried. We joked about being frog-girls compared to Sandy and her group. Candi pointed out how happy frogs were and put her hand around my shoulder. She said she'd be happy to protect my reputation in high school. I didn't know then, but my life would depend on her.

Twenty-three

California Girls

Candi and I met the Beach Boys over spring break in our sopho-more year. Or, to be accurate, jumped and screamed, underage, in a beer-soaked crowd at this earth-shattering show. We stayed in a perfectly dingy beachside apartment in Newport Beach, loosely supervised by her mother, Madelon, the head of our high school English department. One night, we clever girls threw her off with a likely story and walked into the pulsing night of beach town life.

Caught in the glow of the street lights, particles of water danced in the air like tiny fairies. Cruising cars boomed KFWB, the rock station we loved, as they rolled slowly up and down Balboa Blvd. The boys and girls hanging out the car windows were loud, taunting, and laughing. Beer-fueled boys draped over apartment balconies, whistled, and called out to girls, begging them to come up and party. We watched, soaking in the entire scene of spring break, wishing to be older.

Candi and I were lightly sunburned, the first step in achieving a fantastic tan. The two of us were precise about the process of tan-ning. It took the right amount of sun in 15-minute increments at every angle to perfect a ratio of even tanned skin and bikini line. Perfectly achieved, we would be ready for our "Gidget" perfect entrance to 15th Street in Newport Beach by summer vacation.

But, we were dangerously young.

Candi and I probably flirted our way past the ID check straight into the Rendezvous Ballroom in Newport Beach. I don't have any memory of being stopped and questioned. I do remember the ability to get in, underage, throughout my teens. At the time, I didn't recognize this as a superpower.

The band formed in a garage in Hawthorne, an inland, middle-class town, and was good enough to make it to the Rendezvous Ballroom in Newport. We stood in a crowd, acting older and sipping the beers we conned from cute boys, and watched as the band came onto the stage. We fended off groping hands because we were good girls, smug and satisfied with our skill. The ability to con young men into buying beer was dangerous, but we were daring.

"Hey, cute girl." A hand arrived on the butt or too far around the shoulders.

"Hi there, how about a beer?" Even if they hesitated, they were easily "winked" into thinking it was okay. Beer in hand, we'd act as if it was harmless. No promises were made as we scooted away and into the crowd.

The band set up their equipment, the music started, and we knew — at that precise moment — we were witnessing history. Standing on a floor covered with spilled beer and ground-out cigarettes surrounded by screaming kids, we felt like fireworks had been ignited right on top of us. We lost ourselves in place and time, transported to the special place teenagers go when the sound is right, and the place is full. The Beach Boys were ours forever.

I don't know how we hid the smell of spilled beer and cigarettes in our hair and on our clothes. But no one asked. We could barely sleep, so high on life and too many beers for our young selves. Getting up late the next morning, all showered and damp, we excitedly shared the thrill of the night with Madelon. She was permissive and didn't confront us with any crucial parental correction. As we shared, she, a bit hungover herself, announced we might have reached nirvana. This term was defined over a pot of hot coffee and sweet rolls. Madelon warmed to the conversation, asking questions while Candi and I, glancing at each other, ignored the finer points about the evening. We fell gently into our special teen confidence.

The following November, as Candi and I were giggling in our classroom, perfectly golden pre-tanned juniors, the voice of our principal came across the speaker. John F. Kennedy, the President of the United States, had been shot. We were muted.

Almost immediately, the new U.S. President Lyndon B. Johnson confirmed the United States would continue the Vietnam War. The debate topic was *"Resolved: That the non-communist nations of the world should establish an economic community."* All arguments revolved around our involvement in the war against Communism in Vietnam. Suddenly, we were sobered. I remembered our 2nd-grade pledge to stand strong in the face of the Soviets and standing firm at a debate contest in Riverside, I still felt helpless.

When I look at the pictures of my mother and her friends just after their High School Graduation in the '40s, they looked happy and free of care, just like us. They knew college was their destination, just like us. They had no idea about the horror of the looming war, just like us. Mom's dear childhood friends, the captain of the football team, the chemistry wizard, and the homecoming king, would be sent to war, just like us. In 1964, we sat in, marched, and cried to end the war. We were ignorant that summer. The boys who went to war early in Vietnam were our friends, older brothers and classmates. Now, for no reason we could fathom, the beloved President was assassinated.

Our tears were simply grass in a field, swaying in the wind, no option, no choice, and no power to change anything. Life walked on.

Our California Girl summer suddenly came to an end.

Twenty-four

You Would Cry Too

The Party

We had the summer of 1964 ahead of us. I told my parents I'd be spending the night at Candi's, and I'd call in the morning to let them know we were okay. We had a car, cash, and freedom. Carefree, we were excited to see the cool local band we'd heard about.

I was always a little nervous when we went to a party in a house when the parents were out of town. I knew it was risky, but I'd heard how much fun other girls had. I wasn't very excited about drinking. We'd met drunk guys who got bold and pushy with drunk girls and found it was much easier to fend them off when sipping just one beer.

As we walked through the front door of this modern house into a smoke-filled living room, we were watched with sly glances and whispers. We were the girls from the other side of town. We owned our special cuteness and loved the head-turning buzz as we made our way to the kitchen. We each took a cold beer and reviewed the house decor. It had very weird wallpaper, funny light fixtures, and shag carpet. Snobby, self-absorbed, judgmental girls from the other side of town, we thought we had taste.

The band was great and played way too loud for the space. It was perfect. Our typical exercise was to pick the cute guy in the band. I noticed the dark-haired drummer with smoky eyes, and Candi liked the blond grinning bass player. Our snickering, conspiratorial conversation was covered by noise, so no one could hear anyone talking. Everyone danced close to each other and spilled drips of drinks and ashes on the yellow shag carpet.

Later, when the energy fell away, and people were in various stages of passed out, weaving, and leaving, I looked for my girlfriend. Standing in front of a door in the hallway wallpapered with a strange pattern of tall trees, it looked like the decorator of this mess must have thought walking to your room through a wallpapered forest was a cool thing to do. As I lifted my hand to knock on the door, a low voice came over my shoulder into my ear, "Hey, cute girl."

The drummer was tall and leaning over me. He didn't seem drunk. My brain got fuzzy with his beauty, his heat, his smell, and the coolness of his voice.

I was flattered to be the one he chose. I didn't know then what his choice meant.

"Want to dance with me, pretty one?" His voice was like warm chocolate sauce.

I said, "Uh, sure," in my young girl voice.

I didn't recognize myself as he wrapped his tall body around me and slipped into the kisses of the dance and the music. The feeling was indescribable, and he smelled like nothing I'd ever experienced. My body reacted like it wanted more, and the time to leave came and went. When I broke out of the spell, took a breath, and came to my senses, I clumsily moved out of his arms. I had to find my friend. I moved back down the forest in the hallway to find her. I knocked on the door, and there was no movement or reply, so I walked into the bathroom. As I turned and started back down the hall, the drummer grabbed me.

"I have to go. It's time for us to leave. I have to find my friend." Panic seeped into my voice. I wanted to sound definite and strong, but the sound came out like a mouse.

He kissed me hard and held my hands behind my back as he moved his body on my body into a room. A thought flew across my mind. He'd lied to me, or someone had. This wasn't supposed to happen. I tried hard to twist myself around him and out the door. I tasted blood. He laughed and lifted me onto a large bed. Two hands grabbed my hands and tied them with something. As I twisted and screamed, two other hands grabbed my feet as the drummer shoved my skirt up and pulled my blouse apart. Another boy put his hand over my mouth and laughed.

My mind left as they did what they wanted, over and over again. My tears dried as I traveled far away . . . above my body . . . and away from the bed . . . into the stars above the trees . . .

Grant Mercy On The Girl

Will God show and give an answer
For sin to fade then disappear?
Grant mercy on the girl midst stars,
Who floats on fog above the trees.
Hopes rise up from praying fingers,
Her young sweet soul, never falling.

Drifting upward, float, not falling,
It might be nice to disappear,
Up to the sky above the trees.
Swirling mist with small thin fingers
And softly float among the stars.
God, move close to grant an answer.

Her mind swirls for "NO," no answer.
Sounds change tune — band music falling;
Fear flows through small, grasped, young fingers,
"Come" he commands, her pleas disappear
Through rough halls of tall twisted trees.
The rock band plays on under the stars.

"Hey, over here" he laughs to the stars.
All tears can't hold sweet soul that's falling.
Please find freedom above the trees
To find God with loving answer.
Scrape. Fight. Pain. Please . . . please disappear.
Twigs snap like thin praying fingers.

Young sobbing prayer on weak fingers,
Dim sight through tears, hold fast to stars.
Don't, limp body, don't disappear.
Their calls rise high, each boy falling.
Soul searching through fog, please, answer.
One lost voice in dense twisting trees.

Search vainly for hope through wet trees;
One small soul, shattered numb fingers
Formed weakly in prayer, please answer.
Is God there, in the mist of stars?
Sweet prayer, sweet tears, no falling
Small soul repairs, tears disappear.
Far above high trees, rise to the stars,

Indifferent to pain, no falling. Thin fingers
Linked numbly in prayer,
God gives answer in swirling sweet mist;
No need to disappear.

My Apologies

The summer passed in a sadness I couldn't comprehend. Caught daydreaming in the middle of conversations, my mom tried on and off to shame me out of my stupor.

"What is the problem with you? What has gotten into you?"

One summer afternoon, we prepared a picnic luncheon for some of her friends. My back was turned to her as I prepared potatoes for the salad. She started to pick apart my plans for college and my career choice as a journalist.

"I don't think you know that we cannot afford to pay for college. We had to work and pay for our own education. There's no free ride in this family. And if you think you will be able to get a job without a college education, you are sorely wrong. You cannot party your way into adulthood."

The pressure of the secret was indescribable. It screamed and clawed to come out. It took every bit of my concentration to not cry, not tell, and act normal. Yet it roared.

A cooled, cooked potato left my hand and hit the back of my mother's head. It exploded as soon as it landed. Knowing my life could end in an instant, I dropped everything and ran up the stairs to my room. I closed the door, sat on the floor, and braced my back against it. She pounded, screaming my full name, "Janet Cathryn Shryer! You get out here right now! Now! Move it, young lady! Now!"

I thought about my options. Facing Mom was better than raising the window and jumping out. Where would I go? I had to stand up and take it if I was going to survive. I opened the door and stood ready. She was there, covered in cooked potato, and as she blinked, bits of potato fell to her chest and flew into her hair. It was so funny that I put my hands over my mouth and started to laugh. And, in a breath, getting ready to slam me with a hand or words, she laughed. We collapsed in hilarity and, through our tears, hugged and apologized.

I almost told her, but didn't.

September 1964

Dear Mom,

I'm sorry I didn't tell you but I never will.

I'd known since I was nine that I reflected your success as a mother. I could not bear to witness your imagined failure. I was too weak to fight; I was blind and ashamed to let myself get into that room. I thought I was strong, but I couldn't . . . didn't fight back.

You still had power over me, and I wasn't ready for what you might do.

You complimented me on my weight loss, and Mom, it had nothing to do with hunger. I was young, hurt, and terrified.

I didn't tell Dad.

He might drive through town with a shotgun and cause a problem bigger than mine.

Mom, I filled the hollow space with silence and locked the top. I added a bow to disguise it. I prayed the thing could never escape. It struggled to get out, and after a while, it quieted down, withered, and slept.

I love you, Mom, and always will.

Twenty years later, before she died, we talked about the potato scene. Then I told her what happened, she wept. "Oh no, my precious girl." Then, with shaky hands holding mine, she shared her story of shame and loss of hope. We were the same, women sharing what's common and should never be.

Twenty-five

Homecoming '64

My senior year started rough. I didn't tell anyone about what happened at the party. I did my best to put one foot in front of the other. I failed.

I lost my homework somewhere. *But where? My god, it's gone. Maybe I forgot to bring my notebook home.* My empty locker stared at me. My mind went wild.

Driving to school one day, I missed the turn to the school. *I have to pull over. Oh God, I can't breathe.*

Later that week, after I'd left campus to get lunch at In-N-Out Burger, I missed the turn to my school, my mind traveling to places interlaced, not fitting with reality. My lunch stayed on the floor of my car, untouched and unseen. I had to pull it together.

I walked through each day, hoping my face reflected someone I knew. Day by day, day by day, the questions persisted. *What's wrong with me? When did I split in two?*

Driving home, someone cut me off, and I started screaming. *I can't stop, I won't stop, I will not stop, I'll scream forever.* Sobbing, I put my head on my arms, resting on the steering wheel, and fell asleep on the off-ramp of the freeway. I woke to a knock on the window. The highway patrol officer asked me what I was doing. *Oh Shit, oh shit, I'm in trouble. How will I explain this?* He wrote me a ticket for stopping for no good reason. I got home and looked at my mother. The heavy, sharp-pointed vest of guilt-love bore down on my exhausted body. I had to pull it together. *Oh God, if she asks if I'm okay, I'll break apart.*

Parents, teachers, and friends could not be part of this. If they asked, I might break. I would have to pay for my weakness and struggled to be careful. The monster secret gnashed its teeth and growled hot putrid breath as it paced around its cage. I had to remember my life will be ruined if I tell. My life will need to end.

At a critical state finals speech contest at UC Santa Barbara, my debate partner yanked me aside in the hallway and whisper-yelled at me to get a hold of myself. I was probably catatonic. I couldn't picture myself. I magically received some awards in the extemporaneous and impromptu speech contests. No doubt, I wept with emotion and fooled the panel in my struggle to find level. My debate partner reminded me that though I might have done okay, she had a much higher score. She'd saved the team position while I barely squeezed by with my minor efforts. Not a good show. I didn't care enough to take the insult. *Shut up and back off; leave me the hell alone. Get me out of here. Let me sleep and disappear.*

My political science and speech teachers nominated me, and I was voted onto the Student Congress as a representative of our region. In a month, we were scheduled to meet at San Diego State College. At practice, I was so upset that I kept getting up and running out of the room to throw up. I was so disengaged that our team leader told me to stay outside and not bother coming back in. I did anyway, but I don't remember contributing very much. We drove to San Diego. *I hate it, I hate I'm here, I hate I'll fail. I wish I could suck my thumb.*

At the hotel near the San Diego campus, we met for breakfast, all dressed in serious clothes, as if we were professionals ready to work. Our team leader kept glancing at me as if he could hear the growling monster secret. We filed into the auditorium and found our seats. I calculated the route to the bathroom from where I sat as my stomach, bound in a girdle, clenched, waiting to burst into a diarrheal explosion. *I want to sleep on the bathroom floor, curled up on cold tile, for a long time, at least until someone finds me.*

I did what I was supposed to do, minimally, barely living within the confines of the universal laws of the physical universe, one small organism fading into the goo, then focusing, and slowly moving forward. *Okay, I have to learn the best excuse to disappear and find a place to escape until I get it together. Practice makes perfect. Hold back tears. Don't break.*

I started stealing my mother's pain pills, one every other day or so, keeping them in a jewelry box. Maybe they would help me disappear. Normal was hard because of my brain, the rape, and the monster secret that lived there. I lost interest in going to college, my place in the social strata, or even in being a good person.

At homecoming, I still had to show up and participate. The new boy was paying attention to me, a freakish girl inside and a normal senior girl barely breathing. I studied math's rules and logic, but my brain came to a screeching halt when faced with a pop quiz. My father called me stupid when he tried to help me with problems, and I agreed. I wasn't upset with his insults because he was right. He said I'd be better off if I were a boy, that math would be easy.

I cried and studied for hours. Mom saw me and took pity. She talked to a math teacher in her school, and he volunteered to help her daughter and keep quiet. No daughter of hers needed a tutor. He played memory games, practiced problems, numerical variations, and I memorized rules and formulas. I passed tests and quizzes and raised my math grades. I looked at my jewelry chest and felt safe.

Normal was hard. I still had to participate in homecoming at the game as part of the school rally squad. My friends were on the court. A new kid, a half-back on our football team, politely asked if I would be his date. While I wrestled terror down into my body, I smiled nicely and said yes. Then, I politely excused myself to the bathrooms, closed the stall door, placed my hands on the wall, willed myself to hold the tears, and threw up. *Act normal — take a breath and act normal.*

The night of Homecoming, my date and I walked to the gym entrance, wordlessly, side by side, not touching. The autumn night was cool and clear, not yet crisp. The parking lot was filled with cars still just a little stuck in the '50s. Girls wanted to shake off the full skirt style and walk into the dance in dresses shorter, straighter, and more fitted. Flats were in that year. Boys had the surfer look, narrow pants, and thin ties. We were almost primal in our hunger to be new, fresh, and informed.

I saw my friends at the entrance through my clouded eyes, and my unworthy heart ached to be with them. I'd lied to my parents about where I was when we went to the party. I didn't tell Candi what really happened. I let my head drop down, thinking about the little box in my jewelry chest. *I have to make it through tonight. I want to be home, with my cat, in my bed, one pill, safe, asleep.*

Shocking me out of my stupor, my date stopped walking, and with a gentle hand on my shoulder, turned to me. He looked at me silently for a while with his head cocked just a bit; his mouth, set in an unusually strong jaw, moved into a small sweet smile. "Thank you for being my date," he said.

A thought fluttered by, its wings singed by friction between life and demise. I might be okay. I might live.

During spring break, my car gave me freedom. I could travel the long miles to visit both my grandmothers. It took planning, begging, convincing, and arguing with my mother, but the vast lake of pain inside my soul could only be lessened by rest in the sweet perfume of my faraway women. Their fervent religiosity was familiar music. I knew the rhythm even though the ring of earnest faith was lost on me. I did as expected in early morning mass and with the high voices of Brethren Sunday.

Home, revived, loved, and ready to try for a version of normal, my eyes began to see again. I laughed with Candi at random absurdities and started to initiate ideas for fun. We shopped and on weekends went to the beach. After school, we sat cross-legged in her apartment and howled at "The Button-Down Mind of Bob Newhart" and the Smothers Brothers. My rally performance improved, I stopped losing things, and my grades shot up.

ꙭ

One Saturday night in the spring, I went out on a double date with my girlfriend, her date, and mine, her brother's good friend, right before graduation. I felt confident. It was a new kind of confidence, one much closer to the girl my friends knew. I drove to my friend's house and knocked on the door. Her father answered. My friend wasn't home. I thanked him and turned to walk back to my car, and my date drove up. He said the other couple canceled. That minor change in plan caused a problem. I was caught — do I go out or go home? Who will I upset? How would I explain?

These questions rattled in my brain as my date chatted and laughed with my friend's dad. Every instant of the drive, with this boy I didn't know, was emblazoned by firecracker-like internal warnings. I thought about reasons to turn around, call off the date, go back to my car parked at my friend's house, and stop this. Should I use a headache, or cramps, or sudden food poisoning? I second-guessed my thinking; I could not pull together the rational stuff I needed to make a decision. I didn't trust myself on razor-thin ice.

We stopped to buy something to drink. He pulled me to the driver's side to get out. He went into the store, and I said I had to go to the bathroom. Instead, I went to the payphone on the outside of the store. I took the dime out of my shoe and called Dad.

I told Dad the movie we were going to see and the drive-in we were going to. He reviewed his standard threat of grisly death by shotgun if the reprobate laid a hand on me, and my heart swelled with love. He'd be home if I needed to be rescued. Dad asked if he should put the gun in the trunk. I told him I loved him, hung up the phone, and walked to the truck.

The boy came out with a six-pack of beer, opened the driver's side door for me to get in. I slid across the seat to the passenger side of the bench seat.

Parked in our spot, he opened the driver's side window and attached the speaker. I was still worried but knew I could jump out of the truck if I needed to. I looked at the passenger door. The handle was gone, and I stopped breathing. Why didn't I notice? My throat closed, I took a sip of beer. Then, I gathered my wits and asked, "What happened to the door handle?"

He looked over as if it was news to him and said, "Oh yeah, I've had some problems with the pins in that thing, and it keeps falling off."

I acted as if that was a good enough answer and started to say something but didn't. I sat contained and didn't move. I wondered if the sound of my speeding heart could be heard over the noise coming out of the window speaker. I tried to watch the movie and declined the offered beer. He said, "You're no fun. You can't stay sober while I get drunk, now, can you? We need to have some kind of fun tonight."

I said, thinking I was clever, "Oh, I just got over the flu, and beer tends to make me sick." The last thing in the world I needed was a beer. The boy moved closer to me, put his arm around me, and tried to drunk-kiss me.

I pushed him away, his breath was sickening. I said I had to go to the bathroom. I waited for him to move aside and get out of the truck. Instead, his right arm held my shoulder, and his left arm shot out, and he punched me in the stomach. Hard. I lost my breath.

This was war. This. Was. War.

I gasped in shock and pain, trying to get my head to pay attention to what was happening. It seemed so slow, as if I were drugged. I took a breath. I gathered my strength, and I pushed the boy as hard as I could. He was surprised and fell clumsily on the steering wheel.

With spit flying out of his mouth, his face moved into a mask of fury. His lips curled back from his teeth and his fists formed into weapons. He hissed, "You fucking bitch!"

I automatically reached for the passenger door handle, and there was nothing. I forgot it was gone. I put my arms up to protect my face and moved my leg to kick him, but the cab was so small I hit the bottom of the dashboard. My attention instantly went to the pain in my foot. During the battle, he'd gathered himself and was frantically fussing with his pant zipper. I looked up at him. He wiped his mouth and lunged at me, pinning me in the corner of the passenger seat. I bucked, pushed, grunted, and threatened him with clenched teeth and open eyes. He looked at me with surprise, reached for his pants, leaned back, pulled on himself, and sprayed me with his climax, groaning like a crazy animal.

I was a mess. As I gathered my sticky clothes, I growled at him, "Open . . . the g.d. door." I bluffed strength, fury drying any tears. "Let me out, you son-of-a-bitch."

He opened the driver's side door and got out, yanking my arm, dragging me lopsided across the seat, and spun me out of the truck. I fell into sudden rain, face-first onto the blacktop. He backed up and drove away with broken speaker wire slapping on the side of the truck. I stood holding my purse, shorts, one shoe, and blouse together under a sobbing sky. I watched the red tail lights fade in the mist as he sped out of the theater parking lot.

Had I won? I think maybe I'd won.

I cleaned myself up as much as I could in a rust-stained sink in the bathroom and fixed my face in front of the defaced mirror. I wiped his goo off my shorts and sweater with weak paper towels, then matched each button and buttonhole, checked every snap and zipper, then stood up straight, and walked barefoot to the snack bar, not caring how wet I was. It added to the drama. Damn, I did win.

The lady behind the counter gave me some coffee to take off the damp chill and let me use the phone. My dad came to pick me up. We laughed about what a mess I was, and I told him a likely story of a bad date and my brave move to leave the bum flat and call my dad. "That's my smart girl," he said.

I won.

I was alive.

∾℮∽

Toward the end of my junior year, my mother reported my accomplishments in a loud phone call to both my grandmothers, a tribute to her mothering of a teenager. She praised my weight loss and school success, marveling at how well I'd managed to exceed expectations. Damn, I won.

Twenty-six

A Flapjack Revelation

We danced our way through the summer of '65, strong and exploding with cute girl energy. We were outstanding, brilliant, and amazing, poised like rockets, ready to ignite and blast into the world. Our launch pad was 15th Street, Newport Beach, the epicenter of cool — surf, boys, sand, and music. Our glistening bodies were tucked perfectly into bikinis, we were tanned a little too much, and we looked like the cover of *Seventeen Magazine*. We were living the life everybody in the country wanted. We danced to The Beach Boy's "California Girls." We knew the song was about us. We were a new, bright, educated generation who could be anyone, do anything, and go anywhere.

We girlfriends were mindlessly dancing in our beachside apartment. Making a super cool move, I tragically caught my toe on the edge of the rug. I fell, and it broke. There went the sweet flip-flop walk down to the sand just a few feet away. The clinic located on the main drag bandaged my toes together as surfers sat waiting to be treated for their gashes and scrapes. I secretly eyed them. Surfing made every boy devastatingly cute and cool. I was offhandedly invited to a party by one of the boys, who had a bleeding cut on his forehead. I flirted and promised to ask my girlfriends. I walked back to the apartment with a limp, hoping it looked like a surfing injury.

I knew the two-week beach trip would be short for me. How dare my parents insist on taking our last camping trip during this perfect and amazing summer? This summer that existed for the tiniest, once-in-a-lifetime instant in the vortex of every American teen dream? The only summer between high school and college I would ever have again, and I was forced to spend it with these people.

Did they have to honk? Really? Candi and I looked out the window and watched as the car and trailer parked at the curb. Out stepped my parents. Mom posed, slim and athletic, in pedal pushers, cat-eye sunglasses, and a scarf artfully tied around her carefully crafted hair. She was glamorous and embarrassing. My dad was still tall, dark, and handsome. He'd be romantic and mysterious if he didn't speak. This costumed duo arrived to pick me up, dressed like they were in a movie.

My mother waved up to our apartment way too dramatically. Candi said sarcastically, "Oh my, but your mother has arrived in style." Not cool. My friends ran downstairs with my things and prevented the royal couple from coming upstairs and ruining our space. As dad loaded my stuff into the trunk, my girlfriends and I hugged and vowed to see each other soon.

This trip was the California History trip: From Newport to the Oregon border on the coast, then, down through the central Gold Country to Yosemite and Sequoia, topped by a visit with my grandparents at The Ranch in Central California.

As Dad configured the back seat, my mother said in upper tones like some bird, "Off we go!"

Oh, dear God, off we go. How sad my life is.

My mother found the roads closest to where the coastal explorers would have struggled. Fascinating to some, I was sure. Hours into this day's traffic-filled, multi-stop drive through blistering hot Los Angeles, I finally drifted off to sleep.

"There it is!" I woke with a start.

My mother had found another roadside historical marker. These explorers would stop, no matter how life-threatening, get out of the car with a camera, small notebook, and pencil to annotate the footprints of mission founders on the coast of California. On this treacherously curvy highway, Dad negotiated the car, backing up with high skill and superior cussing. I knew this routine: Mom announced too late, Dad acted annoyed and surprised. Mom mumbled "men" as I sullenly watched the faux-exploration unfold and returned to resentful sleep.

We finally reached Jedediah Smith Redwoods State Park and stayed for a few days. Dad sent me to Crescent City with a supply list one morning. It was a gorgeous drive, and my sour mood weakened. I picked up a newspaper as I walked back to the car, and on the front page, the words "More Rioting in LA" jumped off the page. I grabbed the paper with the supplies and rushed back to the park. We sat around our campsite reading the article and discussing the Watts area of Los Angeles that had erupted in a riot that lasted for days. Dad, the gun-waving Republican; Mom, the soft-hearted Socialist; and me, the newly opinionated Democrat — we drove to Crescent City every day to get the paper to follow the story.

They let me drive as they talked about the implications of the riots. My father and mother were on different plateaus of the social argument, but Dad always ended the debate with volume and cussing.

"Damn it, Ina Mae, if you'd only listen. If you paid attention to what I said, you'd see it differently."

"Dear, we are facing social unrest. Of course, it's racial. Social inequity has grown in poverty. It breeds unrest, lack of trust in the establishment, and it sometimes devolves into mass hysteria. Civil unrest is real."

I leaned into Mom's arguments, tossing in quotes from Langston Hughes, to substantiate her plea for justice. The problem was she saw herself on a polished white podium, pretty high over those less fortunate and brown. But, I saw back to school night when she taught grammar school, as the tiny children spoke in halting English while their parents wept. Her argument was a mix of far-off solidarity and moral righteousness in white shoes. There were flaws in her position, and I planned on digging into sociology and political science when I got into college.

The night before we packed to head east to the gold country, we sat around the evening campfire, chatting and cooking the trout Dad and I caught. We gasped in amazement at my mother's aluminum "baked in the fire" salt and pepper potatoes, and I stopped. I watched them. It dawned, like a missile hitting the earth, that I liked these people. We thought the same things were funny. They talked with me like I was an adult, asking my opinion about the riots and if the Civil Rights movement I marched in would really make a difference. Dad got loud, but it was fun to watch them considering my viewpoints about rights, racism, Ayn Rand, and Martin Luther King.

We got to Lassen National Park in the late afternoon. Unpacking and setting up the tent was tricky at night, and we were tired. We set a campfire and perked some much-needed coffee to round off our long drive.

The tent faced east, so the lightning sky had awakened us early. It was chilly and crisp, just cold enough for us to whine about getting up to make breakfast. Dad generously offered to take one for his girls and make breakfast. Mom and I giggled about sleeping in, warm and snug in our sleeping bags, while Dad cussed at the stove, the fire, and the coffee pot.

He looked hilarious fighting camping equipment that he swore made his life hell. Mechanics were always a battle laced with colorful swear word combos. He had this odd idea that the "thing" needed to be wrestled into submission, broken in, so it worked the way he thought it should work. He called the stove a "g-damned, air sucking, horn dog! Shit!" and we laughed so hard we fell into each other's tear-washed faces.

We hastily got dressed, grabbed the TP, and walked out of the tent. We had to go fast. But there he stood. He was six feet, four inches of spatula-waving, ruffle-apron-wearing, angry-faced, cussing man. He tried to convince us that breakfast was impossible in these conditions. Mom and I bent over in laughter and had to leave for the bushes, quick.

We came back, our dignity intact, to the smell of flapjacks, bacon, and perking coffee. Dad looked proud of himself. Ruffled apron splattered and askew, spatula held at attention, he grinned at us. He had mastered the thing.

As we sat down to the hard-won spread, the clouds parted, and sun rays danced over us. The first explorers saw this, but they weren't eating the most delicious flapjacks in the world.

My parent's last camping trip was the year I was married and pregnant with their first grandchild. Mom kept the trip journal. At the end of detailed budgets and exploratory data about early explorers, she wrote, "Boy, do we miss Jan."

Twenty-seven

My Father and the Puma

My parents decided it would be great for me to go to a local college. Their logic was financial. I could live at home, work, pay for my education, and help with the bills. I had been accepted at LA State, and San Diego State but the cost of their master's degree programs, my mother's excesses, and illness left them without savings. Besides, they worked their way through college without help. I could too.

One weekend, college underway, a wild cat tried to take out my father. That was his story. Dad was in the hills near the local shooting range with his well-armed buddies. These men were high school teachers, out for a manly afternoon of guns, shooting, and stories about power, rights, and bravery. This overweight tribe decided to venture into the foothills grunting and groaning, carrying guns, along with the guts they'd developed in civilian life.

Mom and I were in the family room listening to Dvorak's Symphony No. 9 in E Minor. She was reading her favorite novel, and I was studying for a biology test when suddenly, Dad burst into the house breathless, sweating, and anxious.

"Ina Mae, you should have seen it!"

"What?" we said together.

"A wild cat came off the top of an outcropping and almost attacked us," Dad said breathless, with big eyes

"Were you hurt?"

"No, we got him."

"Where is this poor thing?" I questioned.

"Janet, it's a wild animal, not some Disney character!" he shouted at me.

"What did you do with the body?" I asked, unfazed by Dad's attempt to shut me up.

My mother gives me the "I'm with you" eye.

"We took him to the taxidermist."

"You what?" Mom and I said it together.

"I had the kill shot, so I get to have the rug."

Mom was on her feet with both hands on her hips. I was on the couch, covering my face with a book. I didn't want to see it because "it" was about to happen.

"A rug?" Her finger in the air pointed it at him and fired off the verbal shot — "A dead animal rug will never cross the threshold of this house!"

Her voice rose, and I couldn't help it; I peeked. Sure enough, Dad was scrambling for a response besides "gulp."

He rallied defensively, "Look, I shot it, and I *get* to keep it!"

I couldn't believe what I was hearing. I could only imagine how many panicked gunshots were fired in mad confusion when this poor wild, whatever it was, happened to turn the wrong corner. These overweight weekend warriors could not possibly respond with honed hunter skills to tackle a mountain lion, so it had to be some other kind of cat. Heaven help the poor massacred thing!

A few weeks later, it arrived. A bobcat rug entered our home. It was tragic. With innumerable repaired holes and mended rips in its skin, the taxidermist could not take the terror out of the misshapen, cross-stitched eye holes. My mom burst into tears and ran upstairs. My father looked defeated, the pitiful proof of his brave deed, shot to pieces. I could not articulate a response, so I stayed quiet with my defeated father.

My father's hobby, love, and concern revolved around guns. He spent hours in our garage pressing bullets for range practice. I secretly liked it when he dragged me to the shooting range, and with my youth spent targeting jackrabbits, I wasn't too bad. A guy at the shooting range thoughtfully reminded me as I got ready to leave, "Hey, you're pretty good for a girl."

Dad loved to review safety procedures. He approached them with great military detail and complete dedication to preparing his girls. I think he expected us to respect some kind of obscure chain of command. We listened and tried to keep our faces neutral because he was so funny. Dad taught high school history. He was concerned that some angry student or gang member might come to the house and threaten to shoot us.

One Saturday afternoon, he spontaneously prepped us for the possible invasion. Calling us to assemble into the family room, he said with authority, "Now, if you hear someone rattling the doorknob, you have time to unlock the cabinet, pick your weapon, and load before the guy gets through the door."

Mom and I looked at each other, and she picked up a magazine and responded with a straight face, "Well, thank you very much, my dear. Janet — please, will you listen for the rattle? I'll jump up and run to the cabinet, hand you the gun, and you can shoot the guy."

She went back to her magazine, refusing to stand at attention.

With a sour look on his face, hating the fact we were taking this less urgently than he thought we should, he shouted, "Damn it, Ina Mae! You and Janet need to take this seriously."

"Loren, we are, but look at us!" my mother pleaded. "What are the chances we would do that? Janet will call the police, and I'll grab a shovel. I'll come from behind then bean him on the noggin."

It was too much for Mom and me. We laughed while poor Dad, deflated and mad, crashed around cleaning up his demonstration. Mom offered to make him a sandwich and ice tea. Dad did need to be taken seriously and, since I could hardly suppress my snide remarks, I went upstairs. Mom never let him bring a gun on our camping trips. Her logic was he'd be arrested due to his overemotional response to anything that outraged or surprised him.

"What if you kill a bear or another camper's dog?" she'd ask. Then add, "Or a camper?"

He went out the back door to have a cigarette and talk with Gus, the new dog.

He was indiscriminate concerning guns. He illegally packed and was immoveable on the matter. He told us he couldn't wait for a cop to stop him. When my dates showed up, he answered the door with a shotgun in his hand. No one, except Dad, thought that was funny, especially my dates. Dad was dependable in the rescue arena when a date went sideways, or I got abandoned by a friend who left me alone at a party. But as we all grew older, his behavior and viewpoint grounded in the second amendment became worrisome.

We had to have a real talk about his behavior. I came back downstairs while Mom made his lunch, and we sat down outside with Gus, the dog, and talked.

"Look, you told me I could not go anywhere for college. You told me I had to stay here, pay for my own college fees, food, and rent. You told me you and Mom needed me around to help."

He looked surprised with the summation of my prison experience but didn't say anything.

"If you want that to continue, stop the gun drama with my dates. It's not only threatening, but they look shocked, and your smile is creepy."

My father puffed and went quiet. He offered me a cigarette, and I took it.

He started to talk. "Your mother and I," his eyes began to water, "are on different paths." I could barely keep my mouth shut. He and Mom could not be more alike. But, their dreams had been snuffed out when four children died before or at birth. Their effort to turn me into whatever I should be seemed finished, and moreover, they were done. It dawned on me as I stubbed out my smoke that I, too, was finished, and they needed to start something new.

I was living with two friends who wanted rent and expenses — roommates. I kissed his head, ruffled Gus under his fuzzy chin, and went up to my room. I started to clean, tossing clothes into donation piles and creating a pile to throw away. I got a large trash can from the garage, carried it upstairs, and dumped my childhood.

Mom came in alarmed, "Janet! What on earth are you doing?"

I huffed, my bandana askew on my head, and told her with mock drama, "I'm grown up, and I have to throw away my past and move on."

Her eyebrows arched, and she very quietly said, "Don't. I need you." My heart broke, and I hugged her. "Mom, I'm just cleaning. I'm not moving yet."

We sat on my bed, and she started to tell me the same thing Dad said, "Your father and I are on different paths . . . " I saw them, vulnerable and exhausted parents who could not see clearly.

I went back to college reenergized with purpose. Routine helped me focus on what I needed to do to move on and get out of there. I attacked my undergraduate curriculum and got a job in a restaurant in town. I made enough in tips to easily pay expenses, tuition, gas for my VW Bug, and new clothes — by myself. My parents could survive without my help.

Twenty-eight

Homecoming '66

"Avoid popularity; it has many snares,
and no real benefit."
– *William Penn*

I loved my sophomore year of college. The freedom was intoxicating, and I thrived. I fearlessly took and dropped classes, joined clubs, and played on the tennis team. I would write and sing my way through my first two years, then fly onto a university campus, ready for the challenge. Confident, I became a popular second-year student.

At the beginning of that year, I was voted into a group that would end up being the Homecoming Court, 1966. The process woke up my mother, and she took it very seriously. She declared it was an essential item on her "list" of social accomplishments for me.

After I quit the Bible Club, disappointing my dear friend Pam who'd recruited me, I joined anti-establishment groups and marched against the Vietnam War, for civil rights and free speech. As I protested, my branch of popularity sprouted leaves. I met lots of interesting new people and joined them in pushing societal boundaries. I majored in English, knowing I'd become a journalist, but loved my music department classes. I sang in our school musicals, and with the acapella octet, at events, fairs, and conventions across Southern California. My popularity was building into something that felt unusual, solid.

The group of young women in the homecoming preliminaries had to be nominated by a department defined by an academic major like mine, the music department. When I told Mom, she got on the phone immediately and told my grandmothers and aunts what her daughter had accomplished. I can see her now, the handpiece of the yellow wall-mounted phone, tucked between her shoulder and her ear, followed by a long, dragging curly cord. As coffee perked on the counter, she'd pull down a rose-patterned cup and saucer and then settle in for the long brag.

"I know this is a big surprise, but our Jan has made the first cut on the homecoming court. We all should be so proud."

Of course, the grandparents, aunts, and uncles were thrilled and asked what gifts would be appropriate for this honor. My mother knew social timing.

"Not yet," she said, "We have to see how far she gets in the voting. If she makes the cut, we can shower her with flowers."

We turned in our typed fashion and performance plans to the Homecoming Committee in sealed envelopes at the homecoming luncheon. Our choices had to be reviewed and approved by administrators. We were entertained by a speech designed to inspire us, shining examples of 1966 college women.

As I sat in my seat with matching purse and shoes, I looked around and wondered if we might be the last class to celebrate this outdated ritual, but I banished the thought and loved every word and every minute. They told us the court would be chosen by teachers and students' votes in three events: Q&A, fashion show, and a talent contest.

I was practiced, prepped, steely, and ready. My parents were invested, and this nearly fearless daughter was prepared to take home the prize. I was a little worried when I heard the Nursing Department's nominee had been approved to do a modified striptease for talent. She was ethereal, sexy, tiny, and made the rest of us feel like we were hopeless clods. Who on our uptight homecoming committee could have gone for this? No matter, I was ready to win.

The first step was the open question assembly on Wednesday. The audience was much larger than I thought it would be. I felt confident, counting on my debate skills. I knew, in the depths of my soul, I would prevail. The questions were like softballs, and I was ready.

"What should the school do about student parking limitations?"

"*Should the school budget for a new vending machine quad?*"

"*Should we give time and space for Jewish prayer clubs as we do for Christian clubs?*"

The assembly voted on our ability to speak well in public by raising hands for each of our number cards. I ranked first in the top 5. I was on my way.

The next day was the fashion show. I had three outfits to model. My mom and I adjusted hems, updated sleeves, and repositioned darts. The casual look included slim light blue pedal pushers, with a sleeveless madras shirt topped with an over-the-shoulder pink cardigan and darling flats. The afternoon luncheon creation was a pale green A-line dress with a shiny white empire belt, a woven handbag, and a floral scarf wrapped around the wooden handle with white sandals. The formal was delicious. Mom suggested we alter one of her best dresses, a grey silk confection, off-shoulder with a full skirt. The gloves, shoes, and handbag finished the look. I forgot who I was and felt amazing. Mom clicking the brownie camera was giddy with the imagined prize.

Who did win was the girl from the Nursing Department. She took the competition with a spectacular plunging open back, sequined gown. I was second. When I called my mother, having fallen off the victory cliff, she huffed indignantly, "I thought they had taste!" She was ready to contact the school. Thoughts of the impending striptease fluttered in my mind, but I held fast to the belief we were the best talent.

My co-star David and I met at a school play, introduced by my friend Pam, a concert pianist, from the Bible Club. David's comic performance in *Kiss Me Kate* won my heart, and I knew he was the one to clinch the talent show. The three of us decided on the song "My Honey Bun" from *South Pacific.* The characters are a girl in a baggy white sailor uniform and a boy dressed as a hula girl. My sailor uniform was found at the Navy Surplus store. David's outfit required a grass skirt over rolled-up shorts, a bra made out of two halves of a coconut, a wig, and makeup.

We practiced in our living room with my mom playing the director. She was in her glory. She mapped our moves, and we rehearsed every step. Mom and Pam would break into keyboard duets while Dad worked on making the bra-top out of coconuts. He got into the act with his saw and drill, and we ended up with the right two coconut halves. We practiced like people from the Music Department would. Earnest, dedicated, and diving into every musical detail and nuance, we were sure we would win.

Friday night, Dave, Pam, and I were ready, supportive of each other, glassy-eyed, and jumpy with performance butterflies. The show was in the gymnasium, and the audience was abuzz with spirit and enthusiasm. My parents waited by the phone.

We were eighth on the performance list. The first group included a singer, a baton twirler, a gymnastic performance, tap dancing, and dramatic reading. It was finally our turn. Pam was seated at the piano just to the right of the stage, and the song began.

I moved out on stage, walking and swinging like a silly sailor in a costume three times too big, and started to sing:

> "My doll is as dainty as a sparrow,
> her figure is something to applaud.
> Where she's narrow, she's narrow as an arrow, and she's broad,
> where a broad should be broa-a-a-ad."

David entered stage left, swaying in a silly hula. He played it with as much comedy as he could give. The audience howled and cheered through our performance. Pam got deeply into the music, adding dramatic flair, and the audience was on their feet. I was filled, complete, and as the three of us took our bow, we knew, at last, our performance was the winner.

Then, as the crowd quieted, a record scratched, the lights went down, a spotlight hit center stage, and the theme music from *The Stripper* started. We stopped our self-congratulations, turned, and watched. There stood the feather boa-wrapped, blond hair piled on the head of the girl from the Nursing Department. Her back was to the audience. She reached up to her head, unfasted something, and let her long blond hair cascade over her shoulders and down her back. A hush descended over the gym, and she began to slink, stretch, writhe, and move across the stage to every note of the music. She didn't reveal anything really, but the imagination of every person in the room filled in the blanks. We had just lost 1st place.

I called Mom using the payphone on campus to tell her we were on our way. Hot cocoa and cookies awaited us, the trodden troupe. We recounted the whole scene, Pam playing "The Stripper" on our piano, while Dave and I mimed striptease. My parents screamed with laughter as we dramatically acted out each detail of the night we came in second to the Nursing Department.

When the votes came in the following week, I was on the court of five with the girl from the nursing school. The kickoff was a Father/ Daughter dance on Saturday night. The attendees were the faculty, all the nominees, the court, and their fathers. The dress I decided to wear was the grey dress from the fashion show and, just for kicks, my mother took me shopping for even more perfect shoes. Dad picked up his suit at the dry cleaners, got the car washed, the tires polished, and presented me with a corsage.

Off we went to the rented ballroom for the dance. Each court couple, father, and daughter was called to the floor one by one. Applause softened by gloved hands, murmurs of approval, and anticipation greeted each couple for their dance. It was heaven dancing with my dad. He poured on the charm and was the dad of the night. He twirled me under his huge hand, dipped, and lifted me for effect. The memories of being a little girl in the confident, loving arms of my very tall dad filled my heart.

On the following Monday, we had our pictures taken and at the meeting to plan our part of the homecoming game. The tradition was to drive onto the field sitting on flower-covered convertible cars donated by a local car dealership. The tradition was to wear long, white gowns with long gloves, each dressed as the queen until the announcement was made.

First, we forward-thinking, current, conscious women of 1966 decided to wear different colors, not white. We were excited and inspired.

But, how do we get into the stadium in a new way? Our football stadium was in a valley between rolling hills and separated from our campus. What could we imagine?

Idea #1: "on a hay wagon" — NO — Hay?

Idea #2: "on motorcycles" — NO — our multicolored long dresses and flowers?

Idea #3: "let's do cars" — NO — we don't want the old tradition!

Idea #4: "my uncle flies a hot air balloon at the Pomona Fair" — WHAT?

That was it, a hot air balloon. We'll float over the hill and down onto the field. Fantastic! We would step out to the call of our names and walk from the field to the track on a red carpet, collect our flowers and tiaras then meet our awaiting escorts. It was almost as good as Miss America.

Dad wanted to take me shopping for my court dress. We walked into the little formal shop, and the salesgirl made sure Dad was seated. It was in a hilariously dainty upholstered chair, and they handed him a tiny cup of coffee. While he waited for me to model the dresses, he charmed the saleswomen. I heard them giggling.

I came out in dress after dress, and we finally agreed on a velvet and silk gown in forest green. The skirt was a silk column topped by a form-fitting, scoop-necked, long-sleeved velvet top with petal wrists. Watching me, his only child, a pretty dark-haired young woman, turn in front of the mirror, dad wept.

The homecoming game day was filled with activities, pictures in our day dresses, a luncheon with gelled salad, tea sandwiches, and lemonade. Then, it was home to dress and meet in a secret location for the hot air balloon ride. Dad drove me to the site. A fire was filling the balloon with hot air. Ribbons of flowers attached to the bottom of the basket so when we flew, they would flutter in the breeze.

I looked more closely, and there, in the distance, two of the girls on our court were talking to each other, gesturing and pointing. They both wore white dresses. The next two arrived and stepped out of their cars wearing white.

I was stunned. I felt betrayed, like they'd tricked me, or maybe I missed a meeting, or I wasn't listening. I had no idea what to do. Dad saw what was happening and turned me around to face him. He hugged me.

"They prepared to be the Queen." He said it as if he'd uncovered a grand conspiracy. "I'm so proud of you, honey. Hold your head high — you are the true queen." Standing there in the crisp, late afternoon light of indecision, I saw the man my mother fell in love with.

I got in the basket first, and the four white-gowned girls got in one by one. No one said a thing. A group of girls all in white with one in dark green silk and velvet, and no one said anything? But as the balloon floated into the sky, peaked the hill, and dropped slowly to the football field, the crowd went wild. We were announced, one by one and, because of the cheering and the band, the scratchy announcement, and, because four names were called as princesses, and the last one was me, in green, the whole place thought I was the queen. I got the bouquet before they noticed the girl in white still in the back of the balloon basket.

The girl who was queen, never impressed in any of the events. Not the Nursing Department knockout, not me, but the girl rumored to have a very close relationship with the football team. She did a dramatic reading that she forgot. Her fashion was average. How could this be real? She stood in the back of the basket beside me. As my name was called, we looked at each other; the mix-up in the announcement was scratchy and hard to hear. I stepped off the platform to a standing ovation. I turned to look at her, and she was furious. By the time the officials realized their mistake, I had taken the glory. And as we all drove around the stadium, sitting on the top back of the flower-decked convertibles, I stood out, in green, the presumed queen.

I let the chaos surrounding the error wash over me and did not react to any white-gowned court member who was outraged at me being misidentified. Our choices for multicolored gowns were documented with the Homecoming Committee. Not one of the four could whine to anybody. Pictures were taken, four in white and one in green. Forever.

Twenty-nine

Inevitable

Drinking a beer at a college frat party with my best girlfriend Candi, we hummed the tune. *"Keep young and beautiful . . . if you want to be loved."* We groaned together, laughing about my mother, who sang the 50's tune during my Saturday morning weigh-ins.

The noise of the overwhelmingly perfect Rolling Stones wove the background music for our conversation. It was fall, after homecoming and before our graduation from junior college. Our seats let us watch and comment on the alcohol-fueled behavior of the party. We fended off drunk guys and tough-teased them away. We were settled, confident in ourselves, and positioned to review our past with some wisdom.

We talked about people, sit-ins, and protests at school, fashion, food, the war, Bill and Jeff, the boyfriends we'd eventually marry. We trickle-talked about the near future in college and got to the point I'd been thinking about. I announced with some self-satisfaction, "I did it."

She looked at me with her funny freckled face and said, "What the hell did you do?"

I laughed at her brash response, the quality I loved about her from the day we met. I started to verbally check off my list.

"I got accepted into San Diego State. No LA State for me." I continued, "Two years on the rally squad, made the tennis team and made my mark on the homecoming court. Not only that, I auditioned for and made the Southern California Youth Chorale." I tried to arch an eyebrow and added, "And most importantly, I stayed slim."

She groaned, knowing all about my year's long diet and weigh-ins. I feigned model hollow cheeks, and we howled with laughter.

Candi, my rock of a friend, tipped her beer bottle and clinked mine in a toast and roared, "And she called you mediocre?"

My list of accomplishments was just good enough to give her a script for the phone calls to my grandparents and aunts about her outstanding job as a mother.

Jeff and I worked at a trendy restaurant. On our night off, Monday, April 3, 1967, we went out to dinner at the Northwood's Inn in San Gabriel. After our prime rib feast, Jeff whistled, snapped his fingers, and motioned to the waiter. The young man, clearly part of this play, hurried over and put a dessert in front of me. He said "Miss"as he backed away theatrically.

The dessert was a small chocolate cake with a tiny red ring box cleverly affixed with chocolate fudge. Worked into the decorative chocolate icing, the box was adorably topped with whipped cream and a maraschino cherry. The waiters had reworked Happy Birthday into a happy engagement song.

Inside was a ¼ carat diamond engagement ring. I put it on my finger and said yes, and the patrons clapped. We drove home, engaged, in his black Jaguar sports car.

We planned and laughed about how many years we'd be engaged before we ever got married. Our friends had already gotten married. Not only was the Vietnam War looming over our decisions, but it was nearly normal to marry at twenty.

Jeff and I planned to graduate and get jobs before taking that legal step. He had a job lined up with a manufacturing company with government contracts while attending grad school after graduation. That would put him lower on the draft list and, if we were married, even lower.

I was planning on being a high school English teacher even though I'd looked into something else. Among other things, I interviewed with an Army Recruiter at the job fair on campus. The military's rules and structure were attractive, but the only jobs available to females were secretary or nurse. The recruiter could not wait for me to leave his table. He was looking for young, strong men, not girls. Not one positive note of encouragement, not for me. Post-WWII, my parents were part of a generation of college grads who left the farm and became teachers. The path to teaching was inevitable.

I was glad to be engaged with no prospect of a wedding. We wanted to move away to San Diego, graduate with our Bachelor's degrees, and begin our own life. Jeff gunned the powerful Jaguar engine as I waved and walked to my house. Opening the door, I expected to simply walk in and share my engagement. But at the sound of my mother sobbing, I sat on the couch and waited for one of them to speak. My grandmother Lalan had died.

Lalan had started to get tired. She'd talked about it on our last visit: "My dear girl, I'm so tired." She'd take a labored breath and smile, the word pronounced in her southern drawl, "taw-rd." My parents and mother's brother Everett talked about her retiring and taking it easy.

They made sure she could live quietly in her house in Van Nuys, a suburb of Los Angeles until her fatigue became alarming. Everett took her to the hospital, and she died just six days later. She was 70 years old. The lab tested her blood and determined that autoimmune hemolytic anemia (AIHA) was the cause of death. She never complained, and I'm sure she thought the fatigue she fought for years was just a part of getting old.

The memorial was held at St. Elizabeth Catholic Church in Los Angeles. The funeral and burial in our family plot were in Lindsay. It took weeks of our time. Long stretches of driving hours in silence were punctuated with tears and light conversation. At some point in those weeks, I showed Mom and Dad the ring on my finger, but it wasn't really important to any of us. Maybe it was better for the engagement to just be part of the normal grieving process for my dear, darling Lalan. I think she would have been pleased with my engagement. And she would have loved a wedding, never criticizing my choices though she'd pray I'd convert.

Back at school in LA, Jeff and I went through perfunctory motions to announce our engagement. My picture was perfectly placed and written by my girlfriend's mother, our city newspaper's social page editor. We declared our majors to San Diego State. His was psychology, and mine was English with a minor in political science.

We were looking at apartments when I got sick.

I'd be fine and could handle a cold. I called work and school and told them I'd be out for a week. Carefully, I set myself up with aspirin, water, and crackers, getting ready for a virus war. It didn't improve. I went to our family doctor, the one who declared me unable to have children.

I'd been definitively diagnosed at sixteen. There was no question I'd be physically unable to get pregnant. My uterus was misshapen. My mother was distraught. Though after her long struggle with stillbirths, my situation seemed like a tragedy given to her. She wondered if she'd had a twisted uterus that rendered her unable to bear living children. It reminded me of the "bad feet" diagnosis in ballet.

I didn't have the flu. I was pregnant. We'd have to get married fast. We said our vows on August 12, 1967, in a wedding following Emily Post's rules. It was Presbyterian, no alcohol, no food, no dancing. He'd just turned twenty, and I would be twenty in six days.

I didn't see how things had to be his way, or else. The narcotic charm seduced me into doing what I might never do. The wedding acted as a trigger. It was not what he wanted or how he wanted it, and the "baby problem" would have been eliminated if I'd just listened to him.

I didn't see it, blinded by the "right" choice I made and the life of my child.

I didn't know then; I was marrying the wrong man.

Review Inquiry

Hey, it's Jan here.

I hope you've enjoyed the book, finding it empowering and impactful. I have a favor to ask you.

Would you consider giving it a rating wherever you bought the book? Online book stores are more likely to promote a book when they feel good about its content, and reader reviews are a great barometer for a book's quality.

So please go to the website of wherever you bought the book, search for my name and the book title, and leave a review. If able, perhaps consider adding a picture of you holding the book. That increases the likelihood your review will be accepted!

Many thanks in advance,
Janet Pfeifer

Will You Share the Love?
Get this book for a friend, a PHS '65 classmate, or family member!

If you have found this book enjoyable, or familiar and know others who would find it a good read, consider buying them a copy as a gift. Special bulk discounts are available if you would like your whole team or organization to benefit from reading this. Just contact me at Our Silent Voice, mpjp@oursilentvoice.com and visit my book on www.oursilentvoice.com/book.

Would You Like
Janet Pfeifer
to Speak to Your Organization?

Book Now at <u>www.oursilentvoice.com</u>

Janet and Our Silent Voice accepts a limited number of speaking engagements each year. To find out more about the Workshops: How to Write Your Trauma, or buy the OSV Anthologies, visit www.oursilentvoice.com. To learn how you can bring her message of leading a successful life after trauma to your organization, email mpjp@oursilentvoice.com.

Acknowledgments

To my husband David. You were always there to give me honest feedback and send me back to revision when it didn't work. Thank you for being honest and right, every time.

To Dr. Cindy Childress, The Expert's Ghost Writer and my developmental editor. You are the perfect person for me. You loved the girl in this story and made sure I gave her the best stage on which to shine. I look forward to a long and multi-book partnership. Thank you for calling me an author, long before I deserved it.

Loosely Bound Sisters, Chrisine, Tara, Jen, Wendy, Hadia, and Hae Hun, you are the beating heart of this book. You nourish my center. You called me out to tell my story first. I love and trust you.

My partner Marie Posthumus is a visionary and a supporter of those who doubt themselves. Your support and words made the difference. You are treasured and I love you.

And to those of you at Ignite Press. The world in my story is known by you and I cannot think of a team that is better. Thank you for the secret San Joaquin red carpet treatment.

Donna Johnson, your support and love of the girl in this book gave me courage to continue. *Meander, Spiral, and Explode* continues to be an inspiration for this writer who wants innovation. Thank you for that gift. I love your book *Holy Ghost Girl* and I'm looking forward to being authors together. I love you.

To Justin Jannise: In your poetry class I met my partner, Marie. You asked us to bring our "work" into your class for review. She had a folder stuffed with paper and I had one page. I was in over my head. From that class we collaborated and created Our Silent Voice. I now have something I can call "work." Thank you.

Cameron Dezen Hammon, your class humbled me as a new writer. I gained confidence in the craft of writing. The craft is not easy but the individual has no boundaries in its creation. And in its execution, failure is the gift of learning. Your book *This is My Body* held me word by word, page by page. Thank you for the gifts you know you gave to me, and those that can never be adequately expressed.

Carolyn Cohagen, I learned the most fundamental element of story writing, The Three Act Structure. In this class you used *The Wizard of Oz* as the teaching model, and it was simply delicious. Your class saved my book from becoming a snooze-fest of sequential boredom. My editors thank you.

And Nick Flynn, we've never met but I've read your work. *Another Bullshit Night in Suck City* and *I Will Destroy You* showed me how I could fall into the spell of language, phrasing, and tone. It changed how I thought about writing. We may never meet, but know you've made a difference in this writer's life.

For the writing organizations that taught me how to be a creative writer, I hope to honor your purpose. The challenges, prompts, and my tears of refusal to follow your instructions, are part of the golden experience: learning the craft of writing. Writespace Houston, The Writers League of Texas, The Glasscock School at Rice University, and Grackle and Grackle, thank you. Never disappear, always give your gifts of craft and learning. You are priceless.

About the Author

 Janet Pfeifer is an author, as well as Co-Directing Editor of Our Silent Voice. A former corporate manager and California Quality Award Examiner, she built her career by working with corporate leaders and client companies. She lives in Houston, TX with her husband and visits their children and eight grand-teens as often as they can. The grandsons voted to call her GranJan.

Janet can be reached at: www.oursilentvoice.com/book